Concept developed by

Caroline Clissold and Cherri Moseley

Year 4 Author Team

Caroline Clissold, Heather Davis,
Linda Glithro, Steph King

The Publishers would like to thank the following for permission to reproduce copyright material.

Photo credits
Pages 10-11: insects – Valentina Proskurina, irin-k, enterlinedesign, Allocricetulus, vnlit, ArchMan, Henrik Larsson, Peter Waters, Charles Brutlag, paulrommer, xpixel, Eric Isselee – all Shutterstock; sweets and money box – S McTeir; thermometer – Erik Svoboda/Shutterstock; page 19: Xpose/Shutterstock; pages 20-1: coins – claudiodivizia/iStockphoto; door numbers – defototoberg/Shutterstock; poster –Christophe Boisson/iStockphoto; clock – urbanbuzz/Shutterstock; bicycle – Gena73/Shutterstock; page 29: Wikimedia Commons; pages 30-1: egg boxes – Hanis, WestLight – iStockphoto; bus – Evikka/Shutterstock; bus stop – pavla/Shutterstock; goody bags – design56/Shutterstock; height measure – xefstock/iStockphoto; chairs – Anton Gvozdikov/Shutterstock; page 41 – Kathathep/Shutterstock; pages 42-3: bicycle – PushishDonhongsa/iStockphoto; origami – My_inspiration/Shutterstock; spider's web – Aleksey Stemmer/Shutterstock; pandas – Hung Chung Chih/Shutterstock; Notre Dame – Ttsudio/Shutterstock; page 55: Taj Mahal – Luciano Mortula/Shutterstock; Petronas Towers – spectrelabs/iStockphoto; pages 56-7: calendar – alexsl/iStockphoto; penguins – thp73/iStockphoto; Twickenham – via Wikipedia Commons; clock – Paul Maguire/iStockphoto; page 67: medal – Christophe95 via Wikipedia Commons; pages 68-9: signpost – Jamesbowyer/iStockphoto; cooker – Piotre Pawinski/Fotolia; fridge-freezer – Fotovika/Shutterstock; TV – Piotr Adamowicz/Shutterstock; computer – Luisa Leal/Fotolia; page 79 – Wikipedia; pages 80-1: apple – S McTier; chocolate – Maryna Burnatna/Shutterstock; measuring – S McTier; corn – Destinyweddingstudio/Shutterstock; coins – chrisdorney/Shutterstock; page 89 – XiXinXing/Shutterstock; pages 90-1: calendar – Erik Svoboda/Shutterstock; bus – Tupungato/Shutterstock; cans – Slavoljub/Shutterstock; stationery – Africa Studio/Shutterstock; dish – Dani Vincek/Shutterstock; page 103: sabatex/iStockphoto; pages 104-5: building – Claudio Divizia/Shutterstock; tangrams – anaken2012/Shutterstock; map – Goodwin_x/Shutterstock; chess – karens4/iStockphoto; orchard – Marius Szcygiel/Shutterstock; page 113: tessellations – Dario Sablijak/Shutterstock; pages 114-15: baby – spass/Shutterstock; signpost – SCOTTCHAN/Shutterstock; bottles – GrigoryL/Shutterstock; money – S McTeir; speed sign – Rob Byron/Shutterstock; pages 124-5: cars – RobertCorse/iStockphoto; coffee machine – duckycards/iStockphoto; map – Wikipedia Commons; digital clock – spot-h/Shutterstock; analogue clock – didecs/iStockphoto; digital clock – cromic/Shutterstock; Wimbledon – Spyder Monkey via Wikipedia Commons; page 133: halfpennies – Paul Cullen Photography/Shutterstock; pages 126-7: stopwatch – burnel11/Fotolia; tape measure – S McTier; water melon – Gts/Shutterstock; fruit pie – Viktor1/Shutterstock; tumblers – mama_mia/Shutterstock; money – S McTier; page 143: plaster cast – DawnPoland/iStockphoto; pages 144-5: map – AlenkaS/Shutterstock; fruit – Deyan Georgiev/Shutterstock; picture – dotshock/Shutterstock; picture frame – NataLT/Shutterstock; t-shirts – new vave/Shutterstock; shorts – ConstantinosZ/Shutterstock; child – Voyagerix/Shutterstock; page 156-5: paddock – Bohbeh/Shutterstock; car park – apiguide/Shutterstock; ball game – Snap2Art/Shutterstock; butterflies – Mirek Kijewski/Shutterstock (top), Lovely Bird/Shutterstock (bottom); panda – Arthimedes/Shutterstock; page 167: paper - iunewind/Shutterstock (left), Emiel de Lange/Shutterstock (right).

Acknowledgements
The reasoning skills on page 8 are based on John Mason's work on mathematical powers. See Mason, J. and Johnston-Wilder, S. (Eds.) (2004). Learners powers. *Fundamental constructs in Mathematics Education*. London: Routledge Falmer. 115-142.

Every effort has been made to trace all copyright holders, but if any have been inadvertently overlooked, the Publishers will be pleased to make the necessary arrangements at the first opportunity.
Although every effort has been made to ensure that website addresses are correct at time of going to press, Rising Stars cannot be held responsible for the content of any website mentioned in this book. It is sometimes possible to find a relocated web page by typing in the address of the home page for a website in the URL window of your browser.

Hachette UK's policy is to use papers that are natural, renewable and recyclable products and made from wood grown in sustainable forests. The logging and manufacturing processes are expected to conform to the environmental regulations of the country of origin.

ISBN: 978 1 78339 525 5
Text, design and layout © Rising Stars UK Ltd 2016
First published in 2016 by
Rising Stars UK Ltd, part of Hodder Education,
An Hachette UK Company
Carmelite House
50 Victoria Embankment
London EC4Y 0DZ
www.risingstars-uk.com
Authors: Caroline Clissold, Heather Davis, Linda Glithro, Steph King

Programme consultants: Caroline Clissold, Cherri Moseley, Paul Broadbent
Publishers: Fiona Lazenby and Alexandra Riley
Editorial: Kate Baxter, Jane Carr, Lucy Hyde, Jane Morgan, Christine Vaughan, Sarah Chappelow
Project manager: Sue Walton
Series and character design: Steve Evans
Illustrations by Steve Evans

Cover design: Steve Evans and Words & Pictures

A catalogue record for this title is available from the British Library.

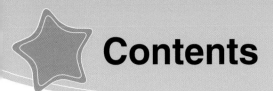

Contents

Introduction

Hello, I'm Ana. Welcome to *Rising Stars Mathematics!*

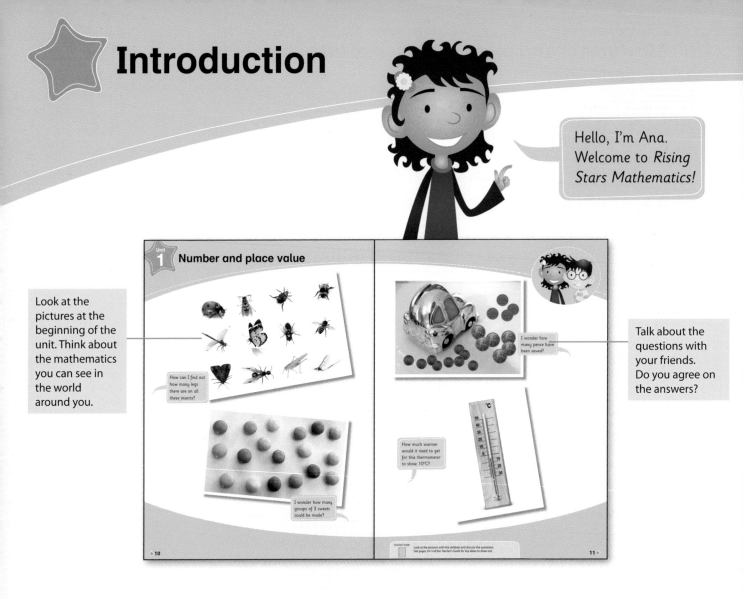

Look at the pictures at the beginning of the unit. Think about the mathematics you can see in the world around you.

Talk about the questions with your friends. Do you agree on the answers?

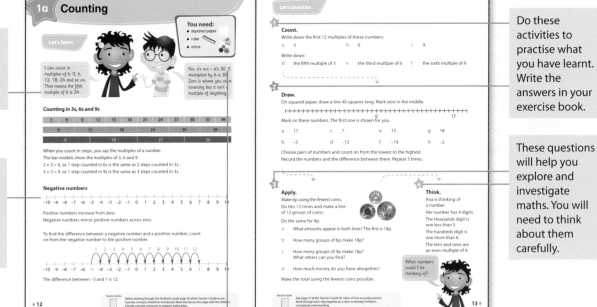

Read what Ana and Tom say. Can you spot if they have made a mistake?

Read the text and look at the diagrams to learn new maths skills. Your teacher will explain them.

Use these items to help you. Make sure you have everything you need.

Do these activities to practise what you have learnt. Write the answers in your exercise book.

These questions will help you explore and investigate maths. You will need to think about them carefully.

And I'm Tom. We'll help you as you learn with this book!

Play the game at the end of the unit to practise what you have learnt.

Make sure you have everything you need.

Follow the instructions to use the gameboard in different ways.

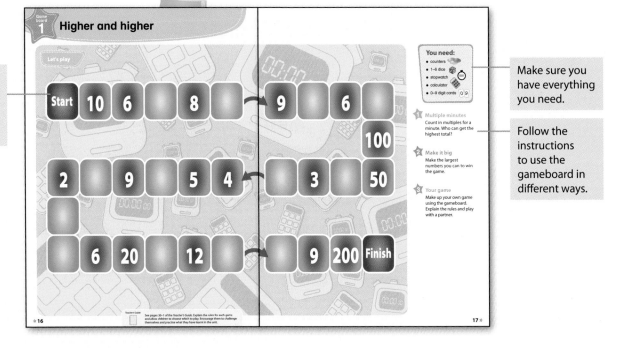

Try these activities to check what you have learnt in the unit. Have you understood all the new maths concepts?

Find out more about maths by reading these fun facts!

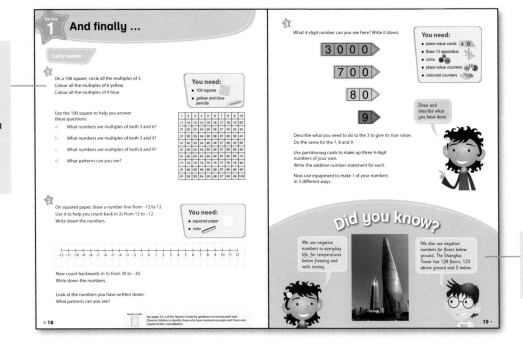

Problem solving and reasoning

Try these ideas to develop your reasoning skills. Doing this will help you improve your mathematical thinking.

Make statements
Can you say what you notice about why something happens?

Convince
Can you persuade other people that your statements are correct?

Generalise
Can you make connections to describe rules and patterns?

Organise
Can you put things into groups, an order or a pattern?

Find examples
Can you give specific examples to fit a pattern or rule?

Classify
Can you identify and name the groups you have organised things into?

Explain
Can you explain your thinking and reasoning about a problem?

Imagine
Can you think of different ideas or ways to do things?

Follow these steps to help you solve problems!

1 Read the problem carefully.

2 What do you need to find out?

3 What data or information is given in the problem?

4 What data or information do you need to use?

5 Make a plan for what to do.

6 Follow your plan to find the answer.

7 Check your answer. Is it correct?
Put your answer into the problem to see if it works with the information given.

8 Evaluate your method. How could you improve it next time?

Number and place value

How can I find out how many legs there are on all these insects?

I wonder how many groups of 3 sweets could be made?

I wonder how many pence have been saved?

How much warmer would it need to get for this thermometer to show 10°C?

Teacher's Guide
Look at the pictures with the children and discuss the questions.
See pages 24–5 of the *Teacher's Guide* for key ideas to draw out.

11

1a Counting

Let's learn

I can count in multiples of 6: 0, 6, 12, 18, 24 and so on. That means the fifth multiple of 6 is 24.

No, it's not – it's 30. 5 multiplied by 6 is 30. Zero is where you start counting but it isn't a multiple of anything.

You need:
- squared paper
- ruler
- coins

Counting in 3s, 6s and 9s

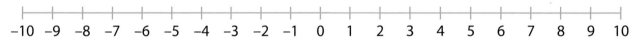

3	6	9	12	15	18	21	24	27	30	33	36

6	12	18	24	30	36

9	18	27	36

When you count in steps, you say the multiples of a number.

The bar models show the multiples of 3, 6 and 9.

2 × 3 = 6, so 1 step counted in 6s is the same as 2 steps counted in 3s.

3 × 3 = 9, so 1 step counted in 9s is the same as 3 steps counted in 3s.

Negative numbers

−10 −9 −8 −7 −6 −5 −4 −3 −2 −1 0 1 2 3 4 5 6 7 8 9 10

Positive numbers increase from zero.

Negative numbers mirror positive numbers across zero.

To find the difference between a negative number and a positive number, count on from the negative number to the positive number.

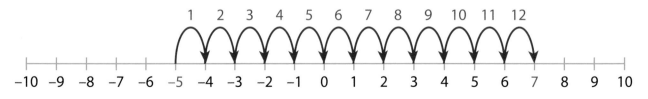

The difference between −5 and 7 is 12.

Teacher's Guide

Before working through the *Textbook*, study page 26 of the *Teacher's Guide* to see how the concepts should be introduced. Read and discuss the page with the children. Provide concrete resources to support exploration.

1

Count.

Write down the first 12 multiples of these numbers:

a   3   b   6   c   9

Write down:

d   the fifth multiple of 3   e   the third multiple of 6   f   the sixth multiple of 9

2

Draw.

On squared paper, draw a line 40 squares long. Mark zero in the middle.

```
|-+-+-+-+-+-+-+-+-+-+-+-+-+-+-+-+-+-+-+-+-+-+-+-+-+-+-+-+-+-+-+-+-+-+-+-+-+-|
                                      0                            17
```

Mark on these numbers. The first one is shown for you.

a   17   c   7   e   13   g   18

b   −5   d   −12   f   −19   h   −2

Choose pairs of numbers and count on from the lowest to the highest.
Record the numbers and the difference between them. Repeat 5 times.

3

Apply.

Make 6p using the fewest coins.
Do this 12 times and make a line
of 12 groups of coins.

Do the same for 9p.

a   What amounts appear in both lines? The first is 18p.

b   How many groups of 6p make 18p?

c   How many groups of 9p make 18p?
    What others can you find?

d   How much money do you have altogether?

Make the total using the fewest coins possible.

4

Think.

Ana is thinking of
a number.

Her number has 4 digits.

The thousands digit is
one less than 5.

The hundreds digit is
one more than 6.

The tens and ones are
an even multiple of 9.

What numbers
could I be
thinking of?

Teacher's Guide
See page 27 of the *Teacher's Guide* for ideas of how to guide practice.
Work through each step together as a class to develop children's
conceptual understanding.

13

Place value

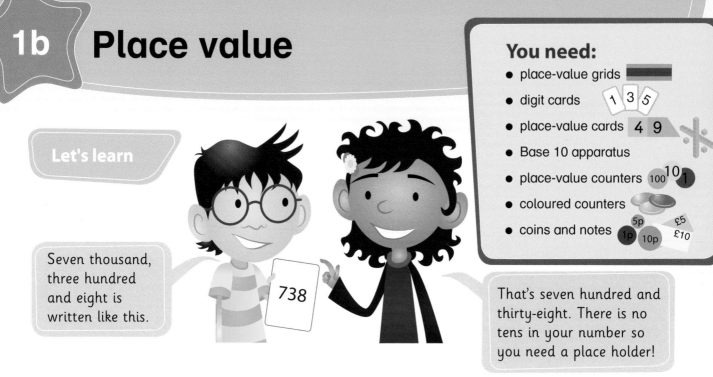

Let's learn

Seven thousand, three hundred and eight is written like this.

738

That's seven hundred and thirty-eight. There is no tens in your number so you need a place holder!

Place-value grids

A place-value grid helps you see the position of each digit.

Look at the grid. 7 is in the thousands position.

1000	100	10	1	.	10th	100th
7	3	0	8	.	4	5

Multiply each digit by its position to find its true value.

$7 \times 1000 = 7000$

Add all the numbers together.

$7000 + 300 + 8 + 0.4 + 0.05 = 7308.45$

There are no tens so you use zero as a place holder.

Different representations

You can represent the same number in lots of different ways.

These 4 pictures all show 1346.

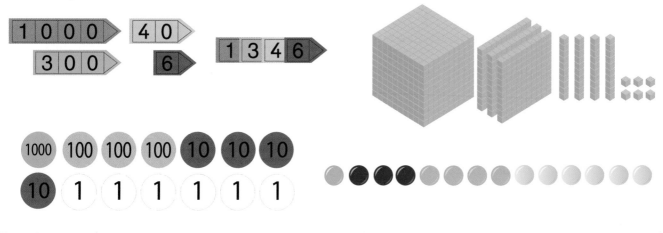

Teacher's Guide

Before working through the *Textbook*, study page 28 of the *Teacher's Guide* to see how the concepts should be introduced. Read and discuss the page with the children. Provide concrete resources to support exploration.

1

Write.

Write down the position of the place holder in these numbers.

a 640

c 2305

e 7630

g 16 070

b 301

d 3025

f 1562.09

h 10 603

Now make up 8 numbers of your own. Each number must have at least 1 place holder.

Ask your partner to tell you their positions.

2

Describe.

Write sentences to describe the positional, multiplicative and additive properties of place value in these numbers.

a 765

c 179.38

e 8352.25

b 628.4

d 2451

f 7819.75

3

Apply.

Use coins and notes to represent these numbers. Use the fewest coins possible.

Record the amounts in 2 different ways.

a 368

c 1050

b 986

d 1281

Write down what these numbers would be if they represented centimetres.

Now write your answers in metres and centimetres.

4

Think.

Use these digits to make as many 4-digit numbers as you can.

Can you find them all? How will you know that you have?

Teacher's Guide
See page 29 of the *Teacher's Guide* for ideas of how to guide practice. Work through each step together as a class to develop children's conceptual understanding.

15

Higher and higher

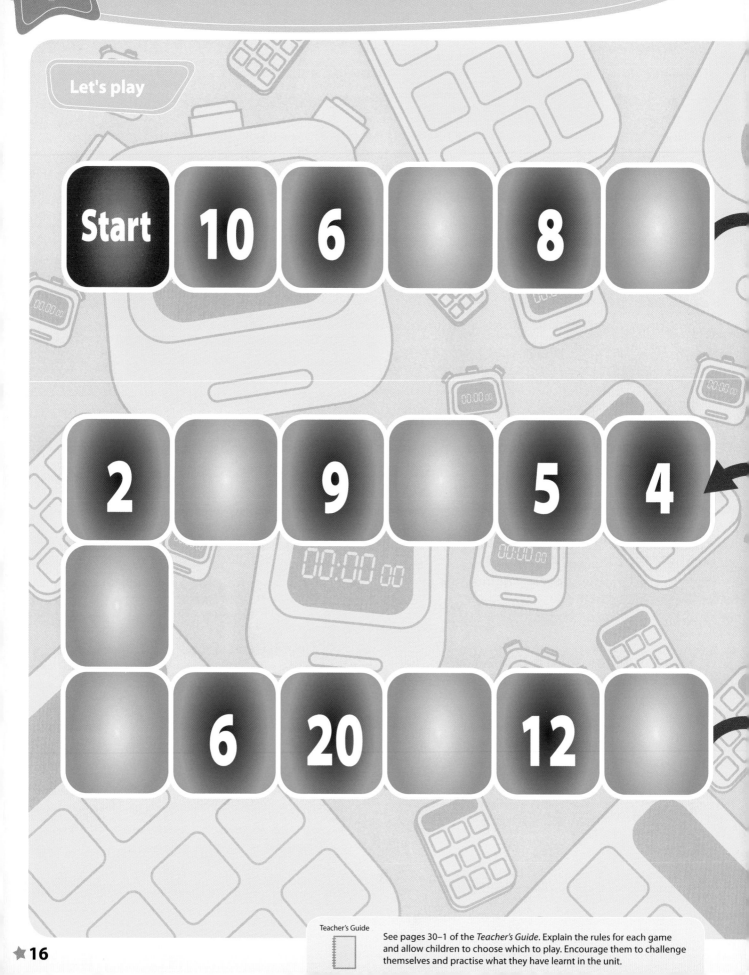

Let's play

Start 10 6 8

2 9 5 4

6 20 12

Teacher's Guide

See pages 30–1 of the *Teacher's Guide*. Explain the rules for each game and allow children to choose which to play. Encourage them to challenge themselves and practise what they have learnt in the unit.

1 Multiple minutes

Count in multiples for a minute. Who can get the highest total?

2 Make it big

Make the largest numbers you can to win the game.

3 Your game

Make up your own game using the gameboard. Explain the rules and play with a partner.

And finally ...

Let's review

On a 100 square, circle all the multiples of 3.
Colour all the multiples of 6 yellow.
Colour all the multiples of 9 blue.

You need:

- 100 square
- yellow and blue pencils

Use the 100 square to help you answer these questions:

a   What numbers are multiples of both 3 and 6?

b   What numbers are multiples of both 3 and 9?

c   What numbers are multiples of both 6 and 9?

d   What patterns can you see?

1	2	3	4	5	6	7	8	9	10
11	12	13	14	15	16	17	18	19	20
21	22	23	24	25	26	27	28	29	30
31	32	33	34	35	36	37	38	39	40
41	42	43	44	45	46	47	48	49	50
51	52	53	54	55	56	57	58	59	60
61	62	63	64	65	66	67	68	69	70
71	72	73	74	75	76	77	78	79	80
81	82	83	84	85	86	87	88	89	90
91	92	93	94	95	96	97	98	99	100

2

On squared paper, draw a number line from –12 to 12.
Use it to help you count back in 2s from 12 to –12.
Write down the numbers.

You need:

- squared paper
- ruler

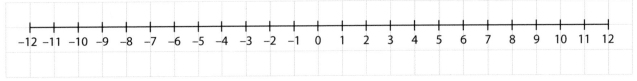

Now count backwards in 5s from 30 to –30.
Write down the numbers.

Look at the numbers you have written down.
What patterns can you see?

Teacher's Guide   See pages 32–3 of the *Teacher's Guide* for guidance on running each task. Observe children to identify those who have mastered concepts and those who require further consolidation.

★18

What 4-digit number can you see here? Write it down.

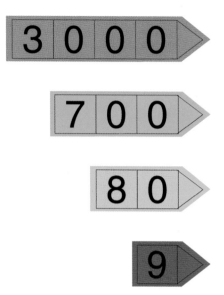

3 0 0 0

7 0 0

8 0

9

You need:

- place-value cards 4 9
- Base 10 apparatus
- coins 5p 1p 10p
- place-value counters 100 10 1
- coloured counters

Draw and describe what you have done.

Describe what you need to do to the 3 to give its true value. Do the same for the 7, 8 and 9.

Use partitioning cards to make up three 4-digit numbers of your own.

Write the additive number statement for each.

Now use equipment to make 1 of your numbers in 5 different ways.

Did you know?

We use negative numbers in everyday life, for temperatures below freezing and with money.

We also use negative numbers for floors below ground. The Shanghai Tower has 128 floors, 123 above ground and 5 below.

Addition and subtraction

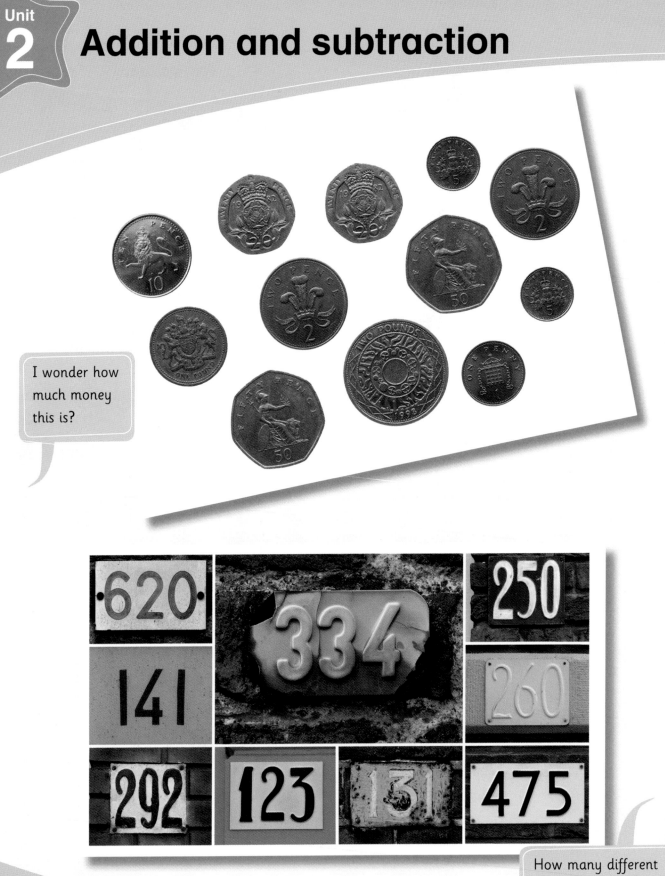

I wonder how much money this is?

How many different sums and differences can you find?

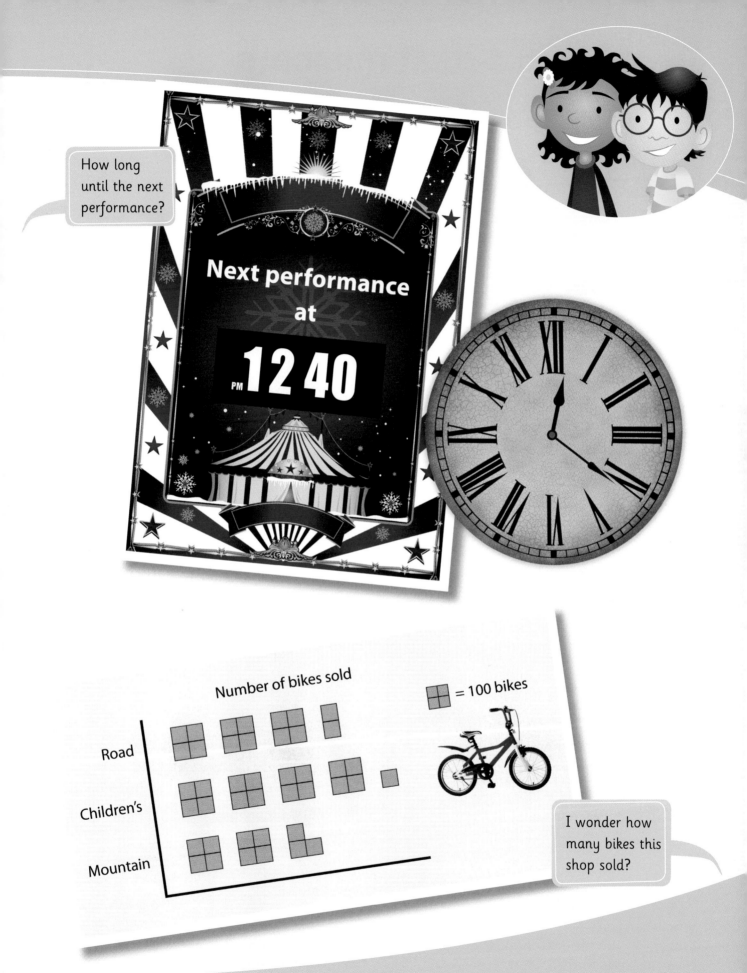

How long until the next performance?

Next performance at

PM 12 40

Number of bikes sold

= 100 bikes

Road

Children's

Mountain

I wonder how many bikes this shop sold?

Teacher's Guide
Look at the pictures with the children and discuss the questions.
See pages 34–5 of the *Teacher's Guide* for key ideas to draw out.

21

Adding 4-digit numbers

Let's learn

When I add together large numbers I must always use a written method.

That's not true! You must always check to see if you can use a mental method first.

Mental methods of addition

2300 is made by adding 2000 + 300. This is its additive property.

The additive property of 4500 is 4000 + 500.

2300 + 4500 is the same as 23 hundreds + 45 hundreds.

1000	100	10	1
2	3	0	0
4	5	0	0

You can use a mental method for adding pairs of 2-digit numbers. Use place value to help you:

23 + 45 = 68
Remember this is 68 hundreds, so 2300 + 4500 = 6800.

$23 + 45 = 20 + 40 + 3 + 5$
$= 60 + 8$
$= 68$

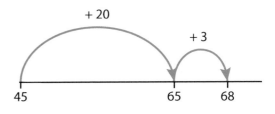

Formal written method of addition

A formal method is more useful to calculate 2378 + 4526 if the tens and ones positions are not zeros.

Estimate first using rounding, e.g. 2000 + 5000 = 7000.

```
  1000 100  10   1
     2   3   7   8
  +  4   5   2   6
  ─────────────────
     6   9   0   4
         1       1
```

Model the formal method with place-value counters.

Where can you see 14 ones?
Where can you see 6 thousands?
How close was the estimate?

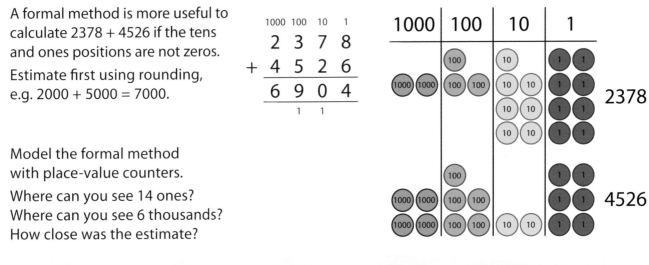

Teacher's Guide

Before working through the *Textbook*, study page 36 of the *Teacher's Guide* to see how the concepts should be introduced. Read and discuss the page with the children. Provide concrete resources to support exploration.

1

Calculate.

Add using a mental method. Explain to your partner how your method works.

a   3600 + 2400 =

c   5000 + 2800 =

e   2060 + 2020 =

b   6700 + 2000 =

d   6000 + 3000 =

f   6007 + 1005 =

2

Calculate.

Estimate the answers to these questions.

Explain why it would be difficult to calculate the answers using a mental method.

a   3417 + 1346 =

b   2374 + 1251 =

c   3843 + 1726 =

Now complete the calculations using the formal method of addition. Use place-value counters or Base 10 apparatus to help you. How close were your estimates?

3

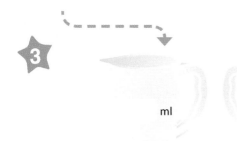

ml   ml

Apply.

Pick 4 digit cards. Make a number. This is the amount of water for the 1st container.

Rearrange the digits to make another 4-digit number. This is the amount of water for the 2nd container.

Calculate the total amount of water in the containers. Estimate first then use the formal written method.

Check your answer on a calculator using subtraction.

> Can you pick 4 different digit cards and arrange them so the total amount of water in the 2 containers is between 5500 ml and 6000 ml?

4

Think.

The table shows money donated to 4 charities. The charities have shops and also receive other donations, e.g. schools collecting money.

	Shop donations	Other donations	Total
Charity A	£5400	£3300	
Charity B	£6347	£2408	
Charity C	£4325		£8325
Charity D			£7800

a   Copy and complete the table for Charities A, B and C.

b   Charity D is given £7800 in total donations. Find some possible amounts to make this true.

Teacher's Guide

See page 37 of the *Teacher's Guide* for ideas of how to guide practice. Work through each step together as a class to develop children's conceptual understanding.

23 ⭐

2b Subtracting 4-digit numbers

Let's learn

You need:
- Base 10 apparatus
- place-value counters
- tape measure
- number lines

In my calculation 3652 – 1437 I have to turn the ones part around to 7 – 2 because I can't do 2 – 7.

No, that will change the calculation to 3657 – 1432 and the answer will not be the same!

Mental methods of subtraction

Always see if you can use a mental method first.

7500 – 2100 can be solved using the number fact 75 – 21 and place value.

Mental methods can be used for numbers that are close together.

2000 – 1878 can be shown using a bar model.

Use the counting-up strategy on the number line to find the difference.

2000	
1878	?

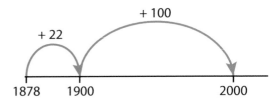

Formal written method of subtraction

To solve 3652 – 1437, a written method is needed.

In the ones column, you cannot subtract 7 from 2.

One of the tens moves to ones position to become ten ones.

You can now subtract 7 and solve the calculation.

Use addition 2215 + 1437 to check the answer.

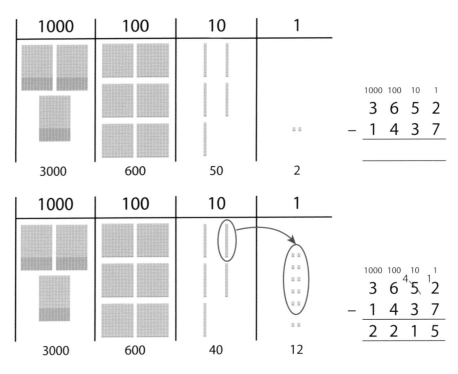

1000	100	10	1
3000	600	50	2

```
  1000 100 10  1
     3   6  5  2
  -  1   4  3  7
  _____
```

1000	100	10	1
3000	600	40	12

```
  1000 100  10  1
     3   6  ⁴5̷ ¹2
  -  1   4   3  7
  _____
     2   2   1  5
```

Teacher's Guide

Before working through the *Textbook*, study page 38 of the *Teacher's Guide* to see how the concepts should be introduced. Read and discuss the page with the children. Provide concrete resources to support exploration.

1

Calculate.

Make an estimate then complete the calculations.

Decide whether to use a mental or written method. Explain why.

a $5000 - 1999 =$ c $4005 - 3980 =$ e $2000 - 750 =$

b $3450 - 1450 =$ d $8300 - 1200 =$ f $2766 - 600 =$

Write the addition calculations to check your answers.

2

Calculate.

Estimate the answers to these calculations.

Now complete the calculations using Base 10 apparatus and the formal written method.

a $4374 - 1263 =$ c $4374 - 1283 =$

b $4374 - 1268 =$ d $4374 - 1563 =$

Write down the different ways you partitioned 4374 for these calculations.

Record each one as $4374 = 4000 + \boxed{} + \boxed{} + \boxed{}$

3

Measure.

Measure your height. Write it to the nearest millimetre (mm).

Measure the height of 2 other children and 1 adult.

Record each height to the nearest millimetre (mm).

Compare 2 heights at a time. Calculate the difference using a mental or written method.

What is the greatest difference in height?

4

Think.

Tom used the addition calculation 3428 + 1385 to check the answer to a subtraction problem.

What subtraction calculation was he doing?

Ana used the addition calculation 2500 + [ ] to check her subtraction.

What subtraction calculation could she be doing?

> Make up a word problem to match the calculation.

> How many different calculations can you make?

Teacher's Guide

See page 39 of the *Teacher's Guide* for ideas of how to guide practice. Work through each step together as a class to develop children's conceptual understanding.

25

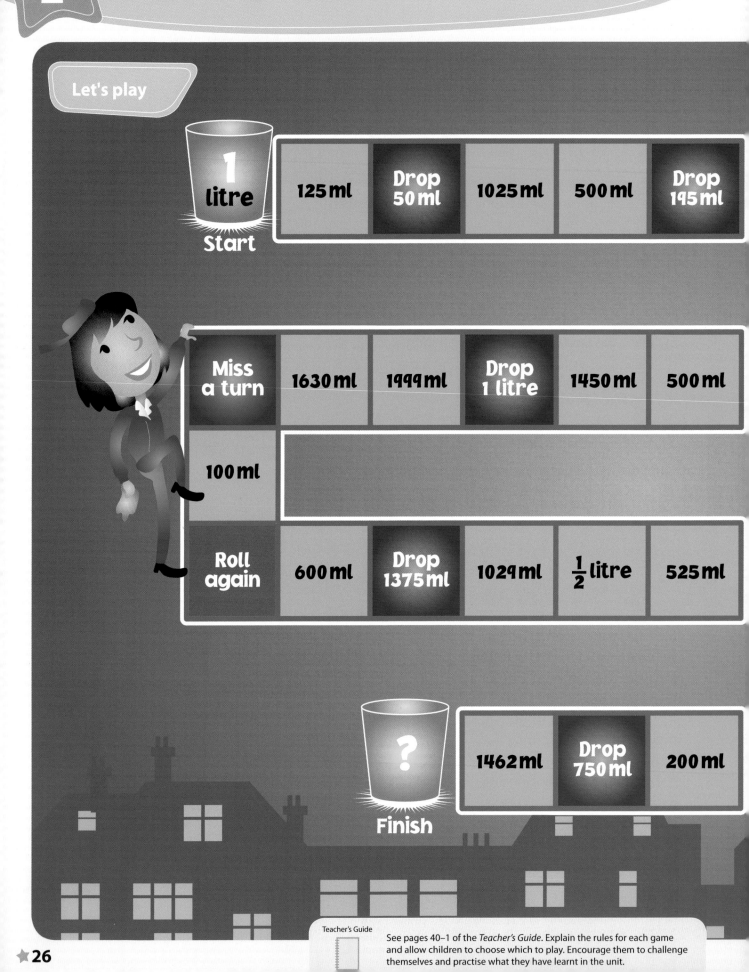

Capacity capers!

Let's play

1 litre
Start

| 125 ml | Drop 50 ml | 1025 ml | 500 ml | Drop 195 ml |

| Miss a turn | 1630 ml | 1999 ml | Drop 1 litre | 1450 ml | 500 ml |

100 ml

| Roll again | 600 ml | Drop 1375 ml | 1029 ml | $\frac{1}{2}$ litre | 525 ml |

?
Finish

| 1462 ml | Drop 750 ml | 200 ml |

450 ml	1750 ml	450 ml	Roll again
236 ml	2180 ml	850 ml	½ litre
			Drop 495 ml

Drop 2500 ml	1000 ml	2168 ml	Drop 1250 ml
			2442 ml
1255 ml	1301 ml	600 ml	Miss a turn

You need:
- 1–6 dice
- counters
- calculator

1 Fill it up!

Race around the track collecting water as you go. Watch out for the drop zones!

2 Drop it!

Try to lose water from your container by making the right choices!

3 Your game

Design your own game using the gameboard. Explain the rules and play with a partner.

And finally ...

1

2140	4744	1700	1999
3500	3000	5002	2200
4375	?	1750	2744

Choose a pair of numbers from the grid.
Make up as many addition and subtraction calculations as you can using a mental method.

Now make up some more calculations where it is better to use a formal written method.

You can add your own numbers in the question mark space!

2

```
  5 6 5 3
-   2 ▢ 4 7
  3 3 0 ▢
```

```
  ▢ 0 5 3
+ 3 5 ▢ 2
  8 6 1 5
```

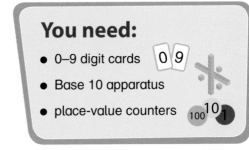

You need:
- 0–9 digit cards [0] [9]
- Base 10 apparatus
- place-value counters (100)(10)(1)

Copy these calculations. Write in the missing numbers.
Prove that your solution is correct.

Use apparatus of your choice to help you.

Teacher's Guide
See pages 42–3 of the *Teacher's Guide* for guidance on running each task.
Observe children to identify those who have mastered concepts and those who require further consolidation.

3

Each month Tapley Town spends money on:

- parks
- outside spaces
- mending roads.

The money spent on mending roads last month was £4795.

Tapley Town spent £1286 more than this on parks and outside spaces.

You need:
- Base 10 apparatus

a   How much did Tapley Town spend altogether?

Remember to make estimates first!

Dalton Village spent £2795 less on mending roads than Tapley Town.

b   How much did Dalton Village spend on mending roads?

Did you know?

In 1949 a mathematician from India called D. R. Kaprekar discovered something amazing about the number 6174, called 'Kaprekar's operation'.

You take any 4-digit number where the digits are not all the same and rearrange the digits to make the largest and smallest number possible. You then subtract the smaller number from the larger number. If you keep doing this, you will always get back to 6174!

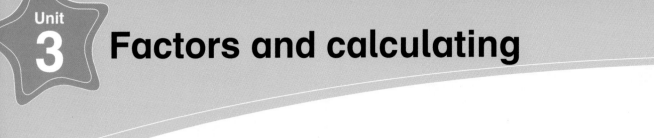

I wonder how many eggs there are in these boxes?

I wonder when the next bus is due?

I wonder how much 9 goodie bags will cost?

I wonder how tall I am in inches?

How many people can watch the show?

Teacher's Guide

Look at the pictures with the children and discuss the questions.
See pages 44–5 of the *Teacher's Guide* for key ideas to draw out.

31

3a Counting in 6s, 9s and 12s

Let's learn

You need:
- number line
- bead string
- number rods

I can count in 9s:
9, 19, 29, 39 ...

You're counting in 10s!
You count in 9s like this:
9, 18, 27, 36 ...

Counting in 6s and 9s

Look at the number line. The black jumps are in steps of 3.

The blue jumps are in steps of 6.

1 blue jump is equivalent to 2 black jumps.

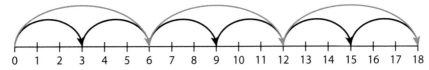

On this number line the red jumps are in steps of 9.

1 red jump is equivalent to 3 black jumps.

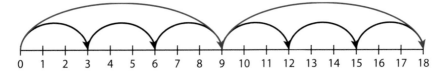

Multiplication facts for 6, 9 and 12

This shows how the multiplication table for 6 links with the multiplication table for 3.

$2 \times 3 = 1 \times 6$ $4 \times 3 = 2 \times 6$ $6 \times 3 = 3 \times 6$

This bar model shows how the multiplication table for 9 links with the multiplication table for 3.

3	6	9	12	15	18	21	24	27
3	3	3	3	3	3	3	3	3
9			9			9		
		9			18			27

This bar model shows how the multiplication table for 12 links with the multiplication table for 6.

6	12	18	24	30	36	42	48
6	6	6	6	6	6	6	6
12		12		12		12	
	12		24		36		48

Teacher's Guide

Before working through the *Textbook*, study page 46 of the *Teacher's Guide* to see how the concepts should be introduced. Read and discuss the page with the children. Provide concrete resources to support exploration.

1

Answer these.

a   Count in 6s from 6. Do you land on 90?

b   Count in 9s from 2. Do you land on 91?

c   Count back in 6 from 100. How many numbers do you count before you pass zero?

d   Count back in 9s from 125. Which single-digit number do you count on?

2

Answer these.

a $6 \times 8 =$

b $6 \times 12 =$

c $9 \times 7 =$

d $9 \times 12 =$

e $12 \times \boxed{} = 48$

f $72 \div \boxed{} = 6$

g $12 \times \boxed{} = 72$

Copy and complete:

h $48 = 6 \times \boxed{}$

i $63 = 9 \times \boxed{}$

j $72 \div 9 = \boxed{}$

What do you notice about your answers to b, f and g?

3

Solve.

a   How many minutes are in 3 hours?

b   A dozen means 12 items. How many bread rolls are in 8 dozen?

c   Ana ran for 720 seconds. How many minutes did she run for?

d   Tom has 72 counters. How many groups of 9 counters can he make?

e   The first bus leaves the town centre at 5 past 8 in the morning. After that, buses leave every 9 minutes. Ana catches the last bus to leave before 9 o'clock in the morning. What time does it leave?

f   Tom reads that depth of water is measured in fathoms. He discovers there are 6 feet in a fathom. How many inches is that? (There are 12 inches in a foot).

4

Think.

a   Count in 6s from 1. What do you notice about the numbers you land on? What if you count in 6s from 2? What is different about the numbers you land on?

Count in 6s from different starting numbers. Explain the patterns you notice.

b   Which numbers appear in the multiplication tables for both 6 and 9? Why is that? Predict which numbers are in the multiplication tables for both 9 and 12. Were you right?

Teacher's Guide
See page 47 of the *Teacher's Guide* for ideas of how to guide practice. Work through each step together as a class to develop children's conceptual understanding.

Calculating mentally

Let's learn

You need:
• counters

I worked out 2 × 9 × 5 in my head.
I did 2 × 9 = 18, then 2 × 5 = 10.
Then 18 × 10 = 180!

That's not right! You only use each number once. 2 × 9 = 18, then 18 × 5 = 90.

Pairing and swapping

Look again at 2 × 9 × 5. You can work it out mentally in several ways.

2 × 9 × 5 = 9 × 2 × 5
          = 9 × 10
          = 90

> Multiplication is commutative. So 2 × 9 = 9 × 2.

> Multiplication is also associative. So you can work out 2 × 5 = 10 first.

Or

2 × 9 × 5 = 2 × (9 × 5)
          = 2 × 45
          = 90

> Multiplication is associative. So you can work out 9 × 5 first.

Using factor pairs

Look at 18 × 5.

18 can be written as a product of a pair of proper factors in several ways.

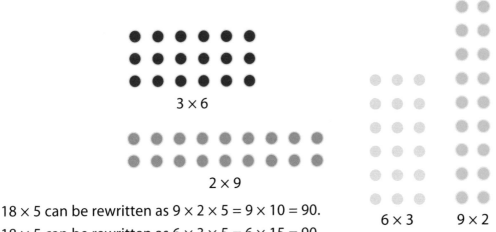

3 × 6

2 × 9

6 × 3   9 × 2

18 × 5 can be rewritten as 9 × 2 × 5 = 9 × 10 = 90.

18 × 5 can be rewritten as 6 × 3 × 5 = 6 × 15 = 90.

This can make a calculation easier to work out mentally.

Teacher's Guide
Before working through the *Textbook*, study page 48 of the *Teacher's Guide* to see how the concepts should be introduced. Read and discuss the page with the children. Provide concrete resources to support exploration.

1

Calculate.

a $4 \times 3 \times 5 =$ c $5 \times 7 \times 4 =$ e $4 \times 45 =$ g $3 \times 75 =$

b $8 \times 9 \times 5 =$ d $2 \times 90 \times 3 =$ f $15 \times 8 =$ h $12 \times 45 =$

2

Write.

Copy the table. Match each calculation to one of the cells in the table.

	Can calculate the answer using 3×2	Cannot calculate the answer using 3×2
Can calculate the answer using 4×5		
Cannot calculate the answer using 4×5		

a 3×75 e 6×3

b 2×90 f 8×5

c 5×9 g 8×9

d 5×16 h 15×3

3

Solve.

a   How many minutes are in 9 hours?

b   How many months are in 50 years?

c   Tom lives 450 m from his school. He walks there and back again each weekday. How far will he walk in a 12-week term?

d   Wooden bricks are 8 cm long. 25 wooden bricks are placed in a straight line. How long is the line?

e   Ana makes paper flowers. Each flower has 5 petals. She makes bunches of 8 flowers. How many petals are in 9 bunches?

4

Think.

a   Write 360 as the product of 2 factors. Do this in as many ways as you can. How many are there? How many ways are there of writing 360 as the product of 3 factors? Explore for another number.

b   The product of 3, 6 and 8 is 144. Copy and complete this table:

$3 \times 6 \times 8$	3×48	18×8
$3 \times 8 \times 6$	3×48	24×6
$6 \times 3 \times 8$		

What do you notice? Will this always happen with a product of 3 numbers?

Teacher's Guide

See page 49 of the *Teacher's Guide* for ideas of how to guide practice. Work through each step together as a class to develop children's conceptual understanding.

35

Calculating on paper

Let's learn

I can work out 9×53 easily. 9×5 is 45 and 9×3 is 27.
Add them together and you get 72.

That can't be right. 9×50 is 450, so your answer is far too small. The 5 is really 50. 9×50 is 450 and then add 27. The correct answer is 477.

Multiplying a 2-digit number by a single-digit number

Look at 6×23.

	23	
6		

Replace the dots in the arrays with their total.

	10	10	3
6	60	60	18

Partition 23 into 2 tens and 3 ones.

	10	10	3
6			

Join the 2 tens to make 20.

	20	3
6	120	18

$120 + 18 = 138$, so $6 \times 23 = 138$.

Solving 2-step problems

Look at $4 \times 3 + 7$.

The bar model shows the calculation.

4	4	4	7
	?		

3 lots of 4 equals 12

12	7
?	

$12 + 7 = 19$

Always do multiplication before addition.

Look at $4 \times 3 + 5 \times 2$.

The bar model shows the calculation.

4	4	4	5	5
		?		

3 lots of 4 equals 12

12	5	5
	?	

2 lots of 5 equals 10

12	10
	?

$12 + 10 = 22$

1

Calculate.

a $6 \times 32 =$ c $47 \times 8 =$ e $58 \times 6 = 6 \times \boxed{} + 6 \times 8$ g $4 \times \boxed{} + 4 \times 7 = 4 \times 67$

b $9 \times 24 =$ d $86 \times 6 =$ f $9 \times 73 = 9 \times 70 + 9 \times \boxed{}$ h $9 \times 80 + 9 \times 6 = 9 \times \boxed{}$

2

Copy and complete.

a $4 \times 9 + 7 =$ d $17 + 27 \times 8 =$ g $6 \times \boxed{} + 3 = 51$

b $9 \times 14 + 3 =$ e $3 \times 9 + \boxed{} = 32$ h $11 + 9 \times \boxed{} = 74$

c $12 + 3 \times 9 =$ f $61 = 7 \times 6 + \boxed{}$

3

Solve.

a   Tom buys a ruler for 75p. He also buys 6 pencils at 12p each. How much does he spend?

b   The engine of a train is 10 metres long. Each carriage is 12 metres long. A train consists of an engine and 6 carriages. How long is the train?

c   A bowl weighs 250 g. Apples weigh 100 g each. What is the weight of the bowl with 7 apples in it?

d   2 adults and 6 children go to see a film. Adult tickets cost £6 and child tickets cost £4. What is the total cost?

e   Ana has 8 bricks that are 3 cm long and 9 bricks that are 5 cm long. She places them end-to-end to make a straight line. How long is the line?

4

Think.

a $6 \times \boxed{} + 6 \times \boxed{} = 6 \times 34$

Copy the number statement, and place numbers in the boxes to make it true.
Do it in a different way.

How many different ways can you find?

Make up another calculation like this. What is the most useful way to partition it?

b

I have bricks that are 3 cm long and bricks that are 5 cm long. I put them end-to-end in a straight line.

What lengths of line can Ana make? How many are there that she cannot make?

Teacher's Guide   See page 51 of the *Teacher's Guide* for ideas of how to guide practice. Work through each step together as a class to develop children's conceptual understanding.

37

Three in a line

Let's play

20	60	90	63	96
78	45	36	54	84
32	12	70	48	81
27	24	99	72	42

Teacher's Guide

See pages 52–3 of the *Teacher's Guide*. Explain the rules for each game and allow children to choose which to play. Encourage them to challenge themselves and practise what they have learnt in the unit.

Game 1

Dice roll:

1 multiple of 3

2 multiple of 6

3 multiple of 9

4 multiple of 12

5 any number

6 miss a turn

1 Know your multiples

Cover numbers to make a line of 3.

2 Multiply it right

Multiply numbers to make a line of 3.

3 Your game

Make up your own game using the gameboard.

Let's review

1

Ana has got her homework questions wrong.

For each question, work out what the mistake was and write some feedback for Ana.

a   Count up in 6s from 2:

2, 6, 16, 26 ...

b $12 - 6 + 4$

$12 - 6 + 4 = 2$

c 9×43

$9 \times 43 = 363$

d 6×28

$6 \times 28 = 60$

e   Work out $3 \times 4 \times 6$:

$3 \times 4 \times 6 = 216$

f $5 + 3 \times 6$

$5 + 3 \times 6 = 48$

g   Work out $5 \times 12 - 9 \times 2$

$5 \times 12 - 9 \times 2 = 30$

2

Show how to work this out in 3 different ways. One of your methods should be an array method.

Which method do you prefer? Explain your choice.

I walked 43 metres around the school field. I did this 6 times. I then walked 20 metres back to my classroom. How many metres did I walk?

Teacher's Guide

See pages 54–5 of the *Teacher's Guide* for guidance on running each task. Observe children to identify those who have mastered concepts and those who require further consolidation.

3

Tom remembers that he used 8 different numbers from 2 to 12 at the top of each column and at the start of each row.

Can you fill in the rest of the square for Tom?

I filled out a multiplication square with 4 numbers in each row and column.
I spilt water over my work! Now you can only see some of the numbers.

×				
			96	
	18			27
		10		18
			32	

Did you know?

12 is a special number.

There are:

12 months in a year	12 tribes of Israel
12 inches in a foot	12 Apostles
12 hours round a clock face	12 Days of Christmas
12 signs of the Zodiac	12 people on a jury

Why do you think that is?

How is 12 special in different cultures?

2-D shapes, angles and symmetry

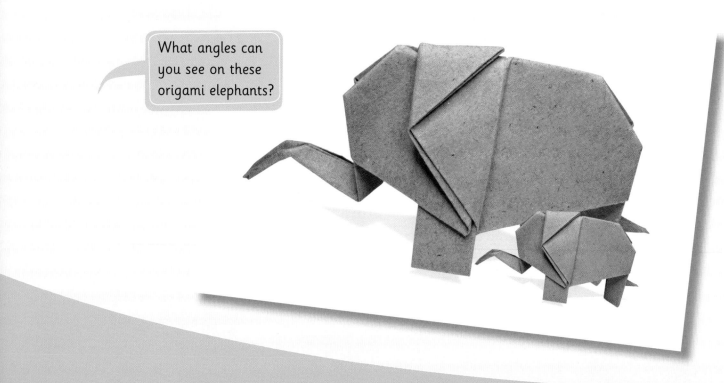

What shapes and angles can you see in this bicycle?

What angles can you see on these origami elephants?

I wonder how many different angles are in this web?

What do you notice in this photo?

Can you see the symmetry in this photo?

Teacher's Guide

Look at the pictures with the children and discuss the questions.
See pages 56–7 of the *Teacher's Guide* for key ideas to draw out.

43 ★

Three types of angle

Let's learn

I can make an angle bigger by drawing longer arms on the angle.

No, that doesn't work! The angle is the amount of turn — that stays the same no matter how long the arms are.

Right angles

Angles are measured in degrees. The symbol for degrees is: °

1 degree is a tiny amount of turn.

1 complete turn is 360°.

A **right angle** is 90°.

The square mark is the symbol used to show a right angle.

4 right angles are equal to 1 complete turn.

Acute and obtuse angles

An **acute angle** is less than 90°.

These acute angles are arranged in order from smallest to largest.

An **obtuse angle** is greater than 90° and less than 180°.

These obtuse angles are arranged in order from largest to smallest.

Teacher's Guide

Before working through the *Textbook*, study page 58 of the *Teacher's Guide* to see how the concepts should be introduced. Read and discuss the page with the children. Provide concrete resources to support exploration.

★44

1 Order.

Find the acute angles.

Find the obtuse angles.

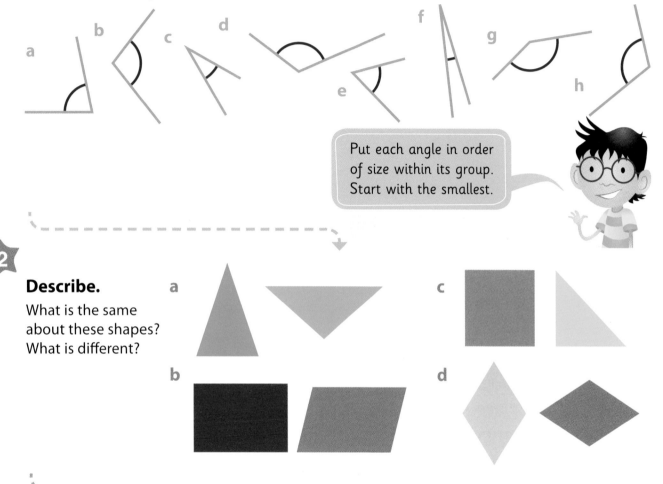

Put each angle in order of size within its group. Start with the smallest.

2 Describe.

What is the same about these shapes? What is different?

a

b

c

d

3 Apply.

Work with a partner or in a group.

Use your body to make acute angles, right angles and obtuse angles.

1 person can make the angle or create an angle together.

Try out different ideas.

Take photos of the best angles.

4 Think.

Draw a pentagon that fits Ana's description.

Is there more than 1 possible solution?

I can draw a pentagon with 1 acute angle, 2 obtuse angles and 2 right angles.

Draw and name 3 polygons with at least:

- 1 acute angle
- 1 right angle
- 1 obtuse angle.

Describe the angles.

Teacher's Guide

See page 59 of the *Teacher's Guide* for ideas of how to guide practice. Work through each step together as a class to develop children's conceptual understanding.

45

You need:
- 2-D shapes
- dotted paper
- ruler
- geoboard

Let's learn

The 3 angles in a triangle are always acute.

That's not always true. Some triangles have 1 obtuse angle – or 1 right angle.

Definition of a triangle

A triangle is a 2-D shape with 3 straight sides.

The prefix 'tri' means 3.
Triangles always have 3 angles.

Types of triangles

There are 3 types of triangles:

Scalene triangle	Isosceles triangle	Equilateral triangle
All sides of different lengths. All angles different sizes.	1 pair of equal sides. 1 pair of equal acute angles.	All sides equal in length. All angles equal (60°).

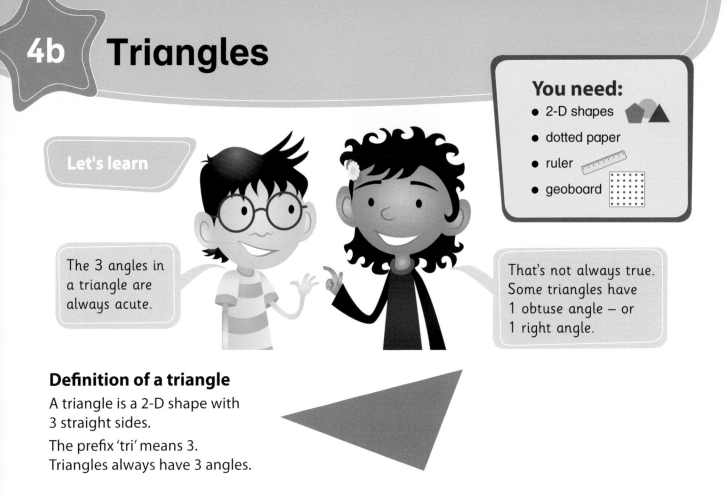

The equilateral triangle is a regular polygon.

In regular polygons, all the sides are the same length and all the angles are equal.

Scalene and isosceles triangles may have 1 right angle or 1 obtuse angle.

Teacher's Guide

Before working through the *Textbook*, study page 60 of the *Teacher's Guide* to see how the concepts should be introduced. Read and discuss the page with the children. Provide concrete resources to support exploration.

1

Answer these.

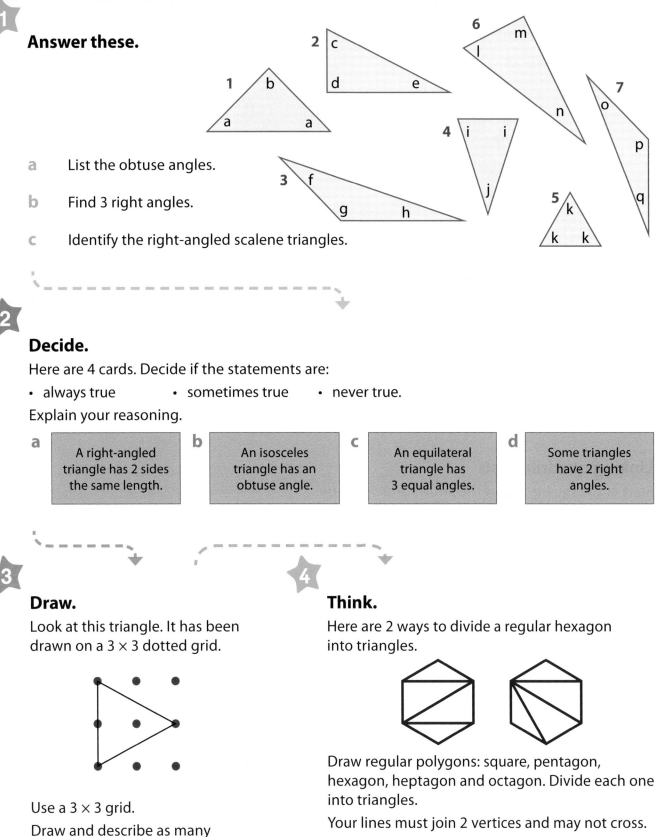

a   List the obtuse angles.

b   Find 3 right angles.

c   Identify the right-angled scalene triangles.

2

Decide.

Here are 4 cards. Decide if the statements are:

- always true   - sometimes true   - never true.

Explain your reasoning.

a	b	c	d
A right-angled triangle has 2 sides the same length.	An isosceles triangle has an obtuse angle.	An equilateral triangle has 3 equal angles.	Some triangles have 2 right angles.

3

Draw.

Look at this triangle. It has been drawn on a 3 × 3 dotted grid.

Use a 3 × 3 grid.

Draw and describe as many different triangles as you can within the 9 dots.

4

Think.

Here are 2 ways to divide a regular hexagon into triangles.

Draw regular polygons: square, pentagon, hexagon, heptagon and octagon. Divide each one into triangles.

Your lines must join 2 vertices and may not cross.

Describe the triangles. Can you spot any patterns?

Explain what you discover.

Teacher's Guide

See page 61 of the *Teacher's Guide* for ideas of how to guide practice.
Work through each step together as a class to develop children's conceptual understanding.

47 ★

Quadrilaterals

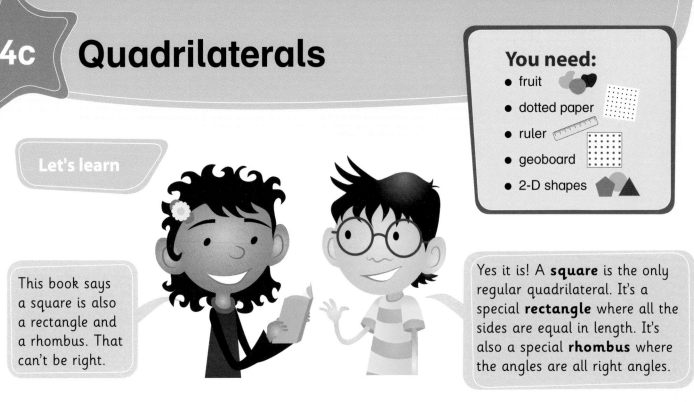

Let's learn

This book says a square is also a rectangle and a rhombus. That can't be right.

Yes it is! A **square** is the only regular quadrilateral. It's a special **rectangle** where all the sides are equal in length. It's also a special **rhombus** where the angles are all right angles.

Definition of a quadrilateral

A quadrilateral is a 2-D shape with 4 straight sides.

Some quadrilaterals have special names.
You have already met the rectangle and square.

Linking quadrilaterals

Start at the square. Follow the arrows anticlockwise.
This shows how changing 1 property makes a rhombus, parallelogram and rectangle.

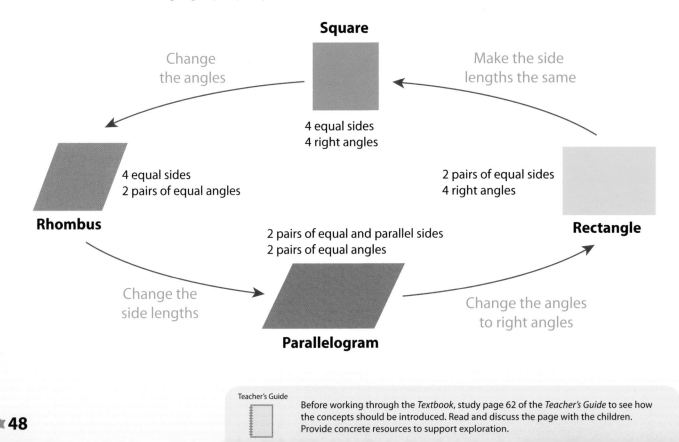

Square

Change the angles

Make the side lengths the same

4 equal sides
4 right angles

4 equal sides
2 pairs of equal angles

2 pairs of equal sides
4 right angles

Rhombus

Rectangle

2 pairs of equal and parallel sides
2 pairs of equal angles

Change the side lengths

Change the angles to right angles

Parallelogram

Teacher's Guide

Before working through the *Textbook*, study page 62 of the *Teacher's Guide* to see how the concepts should be introduced. Read and discuss the page with the children. Provide concrete resources to support exploration.

1

Draw.

Draw and name these shapes:

a   My opposite sides are equal and parallel. I have no right angles.

b   All my angles are right angles. My 4 sides are all the same length.

Write a similar description for another shape.

2

Classify.

Copy this Carroll diagram.
Draw 6 different shapes to fill it.
Put at least 1 shape in each section.

	All sides the same length	~~All sides the same length~~
Quadrilateral		
~~Quadrilateral~~		

3

Apply.

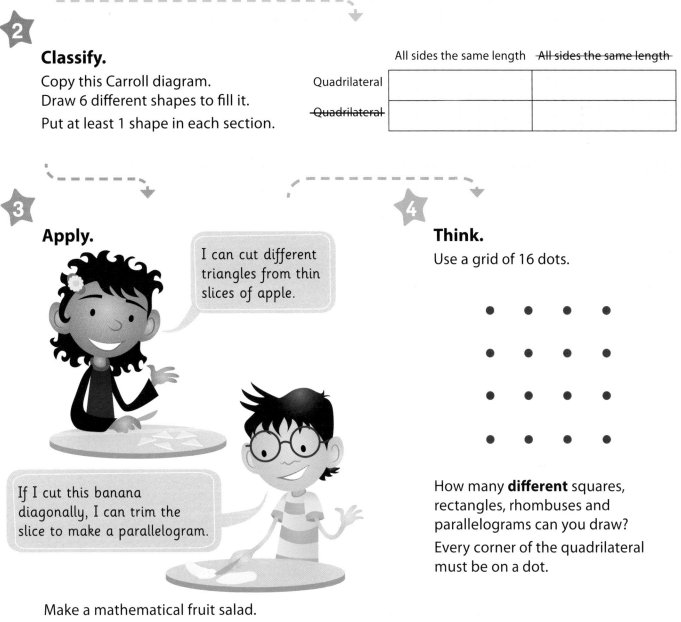

I can cut different triangles from thin slices of apple.

If I cut this banana diagonally, I can trim the slice to make a parallelogram.

Make a mathematical fruit salad.
Include triangular and quadrilateral patterns and shapes.

4

Think.

Use a grid of 16 dots.

• • • •
• • • •
• • • •
• • • •

How many **different** squares, rectangles, rhombuses and parallelograms can you draw?
Every corner of the quadrilateral must be on a dot.

Teacher's Guide
See page 63 of the *Teacher's Guide* for ideas of how to guide practice.
Work through each step together as a class to develop children's conceptual understanding.

Let's learn

You need:
- mirror
- ruler
- 2-D shapes

Squares and rectangles both have 4 lines of symmetry.

You are partly right – squares have 4 lines of symmetry but rectangles only have 2. Use a mirror to check!

Reflection symmetry

In reflection symmetry half of an object or shape is a mirror reflection of the other half.

A **line of symmetry** is an imaginary line. If you fold along it one half of the shape will match the other.

A line of symmetry is sometimes called a mirror line.

A diagonal is a line from 1 corner to another.

Rectangles are not symmetrical along the diagonals.

Rectangles have 2 lines of symmetry. These are horizontal and vertical.

Try folding one.

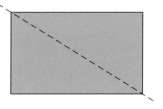
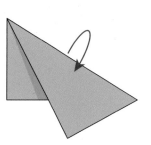
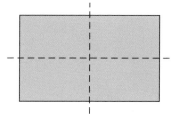

Lines of symmetry in triangles

A triangle can have 3, 1 or no lines of symmetry.

Lines of symmetry can be in any direction, not just vertical or horizontal.

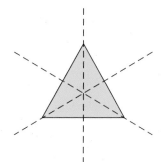
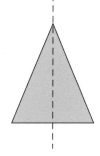
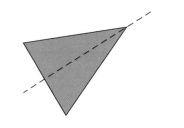

Teacher's Guide

Before working through the *Textbook*, study page 64 of the *Teacher's Guide* to see how the concepts should be introduced. Read and discuss the page with the children. Provide concrete resources to support exploration.

1

Answer these.

Use a mirror to find which of these shapes have:

a no line of symmetry

b 1 line of symmetry

c 2 lines of symmetry

d more than 2 lines of symmetry.

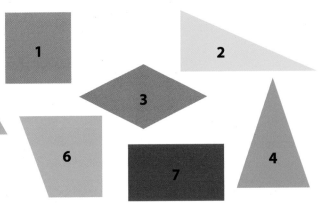

2

Draw.

Draw a quadrilateral:

• with only 1 line of symmetry

• with more than 1 line of symmetry.

Now do the same for a pentagon.

3

Apply.

Copy the table.

Look for examples in your classroom to complete it.

	1 line of symmetry	More than 1 line of symmetry	No line of symmetry
Quadrilateral			
Polygon with more than 4 sides			

4

Think.

Draw around a square.

Mark all the lines of symmetry.

Repeat this for the other regular polygons.

Compare the number of sides with the number of lines of symmetry.

Is there a pattern?

Predict how many lines of symmetry a regular decagon (10 sides) has.

Explain your thinking.

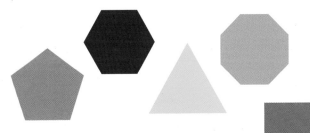

Teacher's Guide
See page 65 of the *Teacher's Guide* for ideas of how to guide practice. Work through each step together as a class to develop children's conceptual understanding.

What's my property?

Let's play

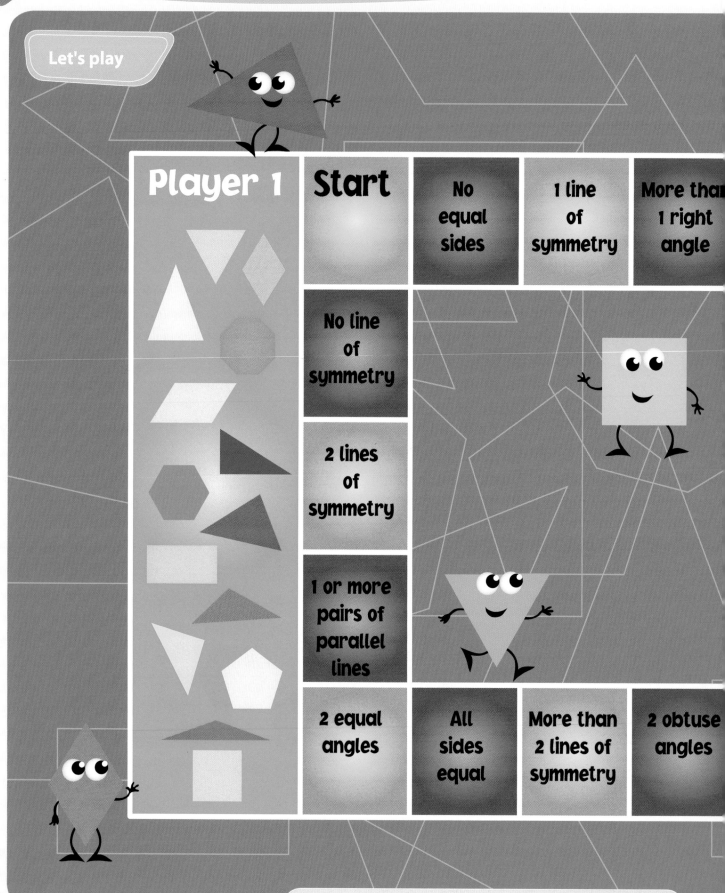

Player 1	Start	No equal sides	1 line of symmetry	More than 1 right angle
No line of symmetry				
2 lines of symmetry				
1 or more pairs of parallel lines				
2 equal angles	All sides equal	More than 2 lines of symmetry	2 obtuse angles

Teacher's Guide

See pages 66–7 of the *Teacher's Guide*. Explain the rules for each game and allow children to choose which to play. Encourage them to challenge themselves and practise what they have learnt in the unit.

★52

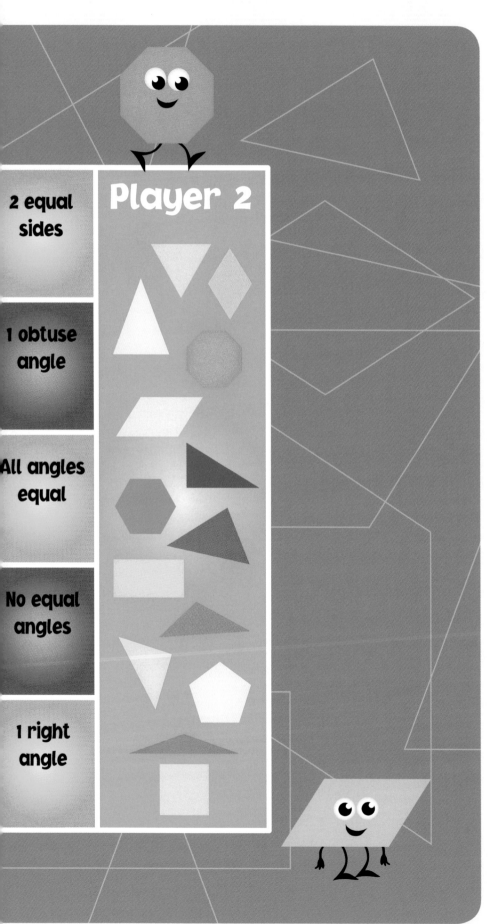

2 equal sides

1 obtuse angle

All angles equal

No equal angles

1 right angle

Player 2

You need:
- 1–6 dice
- counters

1 **Polygon properties**
Match the properties with the shapes to win!

2 **Guess what?**
Guess the shapes by asking careful questions.

3 **Your game**
Make up your own game using the gameboard. Explain the rules and play with a partner.

And finally ...

1

A4 card is rectangular. Each corner is 90°.

Take a piece of A4 card.

Carefully fold 1 of the corners in half.

What size is the new angle that you have made?

Use this as an angle tester.

How can you make an angle tester of 135°?

Use the angle testers you have made to find angles in the classroom.

Copy and complete the table.

You need:

● A4 thin card

You could put 2 angles together.

0° to 45°	45° to 90°	90°	90° to 135°	135° to 180°

2

This clock-face shows a right-angled scalene triangle.

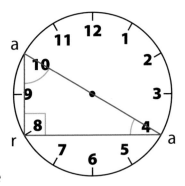

You need:

● blank clock-faces

● ruler

Use the numbers on the clock-face to draw as many different triangles as possible.

Name each triangle. Mark each angle with:

• a (acute angle)

• o (obtuse angle)

• r (right angle).

Now find as many different quadrilaterals as possible.

Name the angles.

Teacher's Guide

See pages 68–9 of the *Teacher's Guide* for guidance on running each task.
Observe children to identify those who have mastered concepts and those who require further consolidation.

★54

3 Sort these shapes according to their properties.
Copy and complete the table.

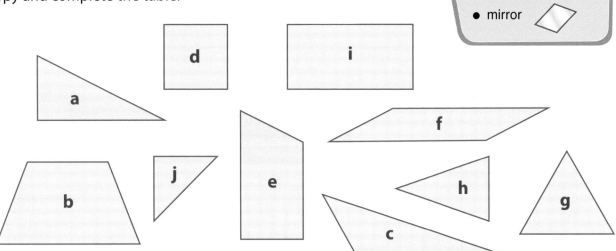

	No right angles	1 or more right angles
At least 1 line of symmetry		
No line of symmetry		

Think of another way to sort the shapes.

Did you know?

For hundreds of years people have thought that symmetrical buildings are beautiful. This is the Taj Mahal, which was built in 1643.

Modern architects also like symmetry – look at The Petronas Towers.

Different numbers

May

SUNDAY	MONDAY	TUESDAY	WEDNESDAY	THURSDAY	FRIDAY	SATURDAY
1	2	3	4	5	6	7
8	9	10	11	12	13	14
15	16	17	18	19	20	21
22	23	24	25	26	27	28
29	30	31				

My uncle is on holiday for the first 3 weeks in May. How many days is that?

I wonder if penguins live in sub-zero temperatures?

I wonder if there are over 1000 people watching the match?

Is there something wrong with the 4 on this clock?

Teacher's Guide
Look at the pictures with the children and discuss the questions.
See pages 70–1 of the *Teacher's Guide* for key ideas to draw out.

57

Let's learn

If I count up 4 from −2, I end up on −6.

That's not right. Negative numbers go backwards from zero. When you count up, you still go from left to right along the number line. Count on 4 from −2 like this: −1, 0, 1, 2.

Counting in 7s

When you count in steps from zero, you say the multiples of a number.

The first 12 multiples of 7 are: 7, 14, 21, 28, 35, 42, 49, 56, 63, 70, 77, 84.

Number bonds help you to count in 7s.

Count how many to the next ten. Then add what is left.

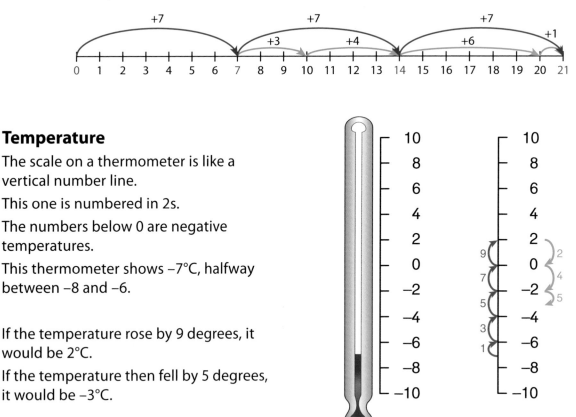

Temperature

The scale on a thermometer is like a vertical number line.

This one is numbered in 2s.

The numbers below 0 are negative temperatures.

This thermometer shows −7°C, halfway between −8 and −6.

If the temperature rose by 9 degrees, it would be 2°C.

If the temperature then fell by 5 degrees, it would be −3°C.

Teacher's Guide

Before working through the *Textbook*, study page 72 of the *Teacher's Guide* to see how the concepts should be introduced. Read and discuss the page with the children. Provide concrete resources to support exploration.

1

Count.

Write down:

a   the first 12 multiples of 7   c   the 5th multiple of 7   e   the 8th multiple of 7

b   the 3rd multiple of 7   d   the 4th multiple of 7   f   the 11th multiple of 7

2

Count.

Write down what these temperatures would be if the temperature fell by 6 degrees.

a   10°C   c   3°C   e   −1°C

b   6°C   d   1°C   f   −7°C

Write down what these temperatures would be if they rose by 5 degrees.

g   8°C   i   −2°C   k   −10°C

h   1°C   j   −5°C   l   −14°C

3

Apply.

Tom is saving money for his holiday. He earns 10p a day doing jobs at home.

a   How much does Tom have saved at the end of 1 week?

b   How much does he have saved at the end of the second week?

c   At the end of 5 weeks, Tom spends 60p on sweets. How much does he have saved now?

d   How much does Tom have saved at the end of 12 weeks?

4

Think.

Roll 2 dice.

The first dice tells you your starting number.

The second dice tells you how many to count.

Count on and back from the starting number to make 2 new numbers.

Write number statements to show how you make your numbers.

Counting on is the same as adding.
5 count on 6 is the same as $5 + 6 = 11$.

Counting back is the same as subtracting.
5 count back 6 is the same as $5 − 6 = −1$.

What other numbers can you make?

Teacher's Guide
See page 73 of the *Teacher's Guide* for ideas of how to guide practice.
Work through each step together as a class to develop children's conceptual understanding.

59

5b Rounding, ordering and comparing

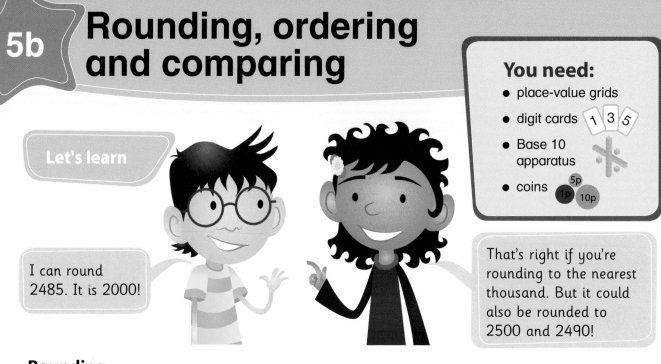

You need:
- place-value grids
- digit cards
- Base 10 apparatus
- coins

Let's learn

I can round 2485. It is 2000!

That's right if you're rounding to the nearest thousand. But it could also be rounded to 2500 and 2490!

Rounding

Rounding is an important skill to learn. It helps with estimating.

4628 is closer to 5000 than 4000.
4628 is 5000 to the nearest 1000.

4628 is closer to 4600 than 4700.
4628 is 4600 to the nearest 100.

4628 is closer to 4630 than 4620.
4628 is 4630 to the nearest 10.

Ordering and comparing

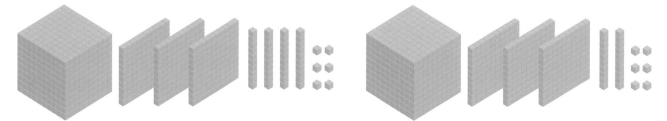

You can use your knowledge of place value to order and compare numbers.

The picture above shows 1346 and 1326.

The numbers have the same number of thousands and the same number of hundreds.

Look at the tens: 2 < 4, so 1326 < 1346
4 > 2, so 1346 > 1326

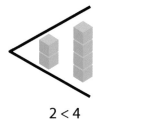

2 < 4   4 > 2

Teacher's Guide — Before working through the *Textbook*, study page 74 of the *Teacher's Guide* to see how the concepts should be introduced. Read and discuss the page with the children. Provide concrete resources to support exploration.

1

Round.

Round these numbers to the nearest 10.

a   246   b   611   c   1345   d   2862

Round these numbers to the nearest 100.

e   768   f   291   g   8349   h   5542

Round these numbers to the nearest 1000.

i   1254   j   4981   k   5499   l   9501

2

Compare. Write 2 comparison statements for these numbers. Use > and <.

a   569 and 469   c   824 and 826   e   2178 and 2148

b   462 and 432   d   1345 and 1445   f   3218 and 3258

Now order all these numbers from greatest to least.

3

Apply.

Make these amounts of money using the fewest coins.

a   £1.35   d   £2.58

b   £1.16   e   £4.12

c   £2.74   f   £3.75

Order the amounts from highest to lowest value.

Take pairs of amounts and make them equal.

Explain the 2 ways you can do this.

My amounts are £1.35 and £2.65. I can make them equal by adding £1.30 to £1.35 or I can subtract £1.30 from £2.65.

4

Think.

Use the symbols and numbers below to make the statement correct:

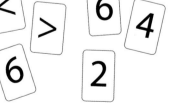

How many different statements can you make? How will you know you have them all?

Teacher's Guide

See page 75 of the *Teacher's Guide* for ideas of how to guide practice. Work through each step together as a class to develop children's conceptual understanding.

61 ★

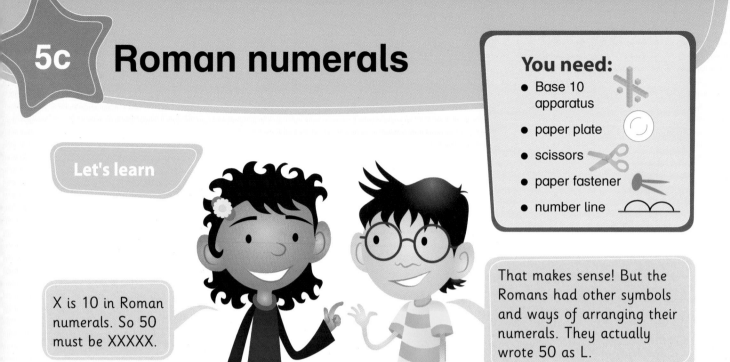

You need:
- Base 10 apparatus
- paper plate
- scissors
- paper fastener
- number line

Let's learn

X is 10 in Roman numerals. So 50 must be XXXXX.

That makes sense! But the Romans had other symbols and ways of arranging their numerals. They actually wrote 50 as L.

Roman numerals to 100

Units	I	II	III	IV	V	VI	VII	VIII	IX
Tens	X	XX	XXX	XL	L	LX	LXX	LXXX	XC

IV means 1 before 5, or 4. C means 100.

In Roman numerals you write the symbol for the tens, then the symbol for the units.

XXXII

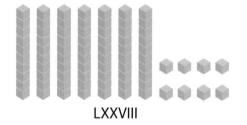

LXXVIII

Partition it into chunks to read it.

Look for a lower value following a higher one.

For example: LXXVIII = L + XX + V + III = 50 + 20 + 5 + 3 = 78

LIV = L + IV = 50 + 4 = 54

Roman numeral clocks

Many of our clocks have Roman numerals.

On this clock, the minute hand is pointing to XII.
The hour hand is pointing to III. It is 3 o'clock.

Teacher's Guide

Before working through the *Textbook*, study page 76 of the *Teacher's Guide* to see how the concepts should be introduced. Read and discuss the page with the children. Provide concrete resources to support exploration.

1

Write.

Write these numbers using Roman numerals.

a	32	c	59	e	94	g	13
b	18	d	75	f	46	h	41

Write down some numbers of your own. Show them in Roman numerals.

2

Write.

Write these Roman numerals as the numbers we use today.

a	XIV	c	XLII	e	LXXVI	g	XXIV
b	XXVII	d	LXII	f	XCIX	h	XCV

Use the table in the Textbook to make up some more Roman numbers.
Then write them in our numbers.

3

Draw.

Draw 6 clock faces that look like this.

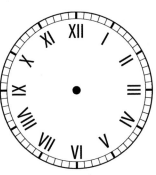

Draw these times on them.
Write the times in 2 other ways by each clock.

a	10 minutes past 9	d	52 minutes past 8
b	40 minutes past 4	e	37 minutes past 11
c	23 minutes past 6	f	18 minutes past 2

Choose pairs of times that you have drawn. Find the time differences between them.

4

Think.

a   Find the Roman number between 1 and 100 that uses the most letters. Write it down in Roman numerals and in our numbers.

b   Use the Roman numerals I, V, X and L. Find the smallest Roman number you can make using each numeral once.

Now find the biggest!

Teacher's Guide   See page 77 of the *Teacher's Guide* for ideas of how to guide practice. Work through each step together as a class to develop children's conceptual understanding.

63

Find a smile!

Let's play

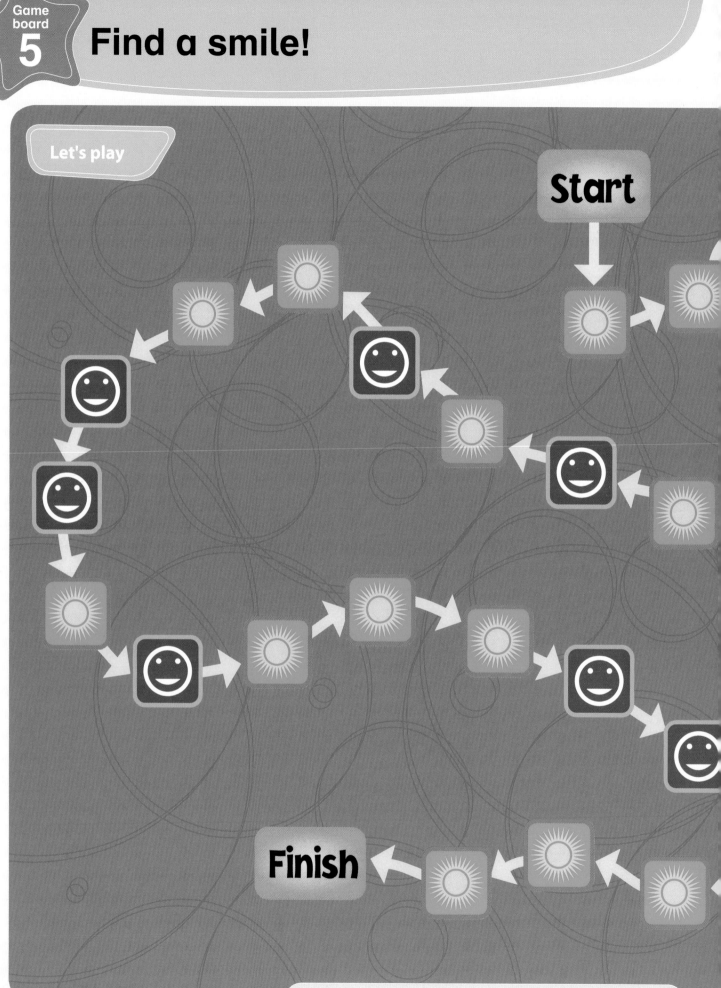

Start

Finish

Teacher's Guide

See pages 78–9 of the *Teacher's Guide*. Explain the rules for each game and allow children to choose which to play. Encourage them to challenge themselves and practise what they have learnt in the unit.

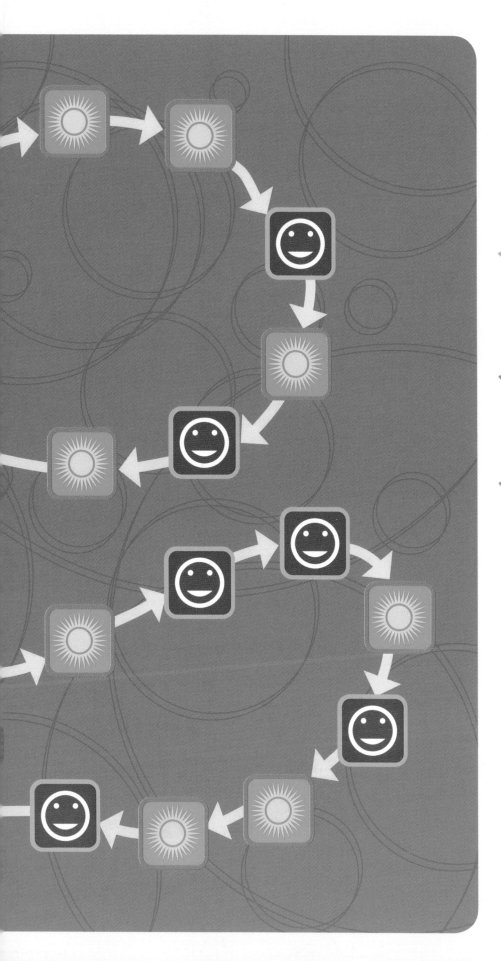

1 Round, round, round

Round 4-digit numbers to score points. Who can get the highest total?

2 Who's got the least?

Make the lowest number you can to win!

3 Your game

Make up your own game using the gameboard. Explain the rules and play with a partner.

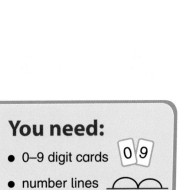

Let's review

1

Write down the first 12 multiples of 7.

Use this information to work out how many days there are in:

a   15 weeks   c   25 weeks

b   20 weeks   d   75 weeks

> Explain how you worked this out.

Start on 14 and count back 5 multiples of 7. What number do you land on?

What if you start on 42 and count back 10 multiples of 7?

What number will be your starting number if you count on in 8 multiples of 7 and get to 35?

Make up some of your own negative starting numbers that are multiples of 7. Ask your partner to count on different numbers of multiples.

2

Pick 4 digit cards. Use them to make 5 different 4-digit numbers. Write a list of the numbers you make.

You need:
- 0–9 digit cards
- number lines

a   Order your 5 numbers from highest to lowest.

b   Choose pairs of numbers from your list. Compare them using the symbols < and >.

c   What can you do to the numbers in each pair to make them equal?

> Now round your 5 numbers to the nearest 10, 100 and 1000.

Teacher's Guide

See pages 80–1 of the *Teacher's Guide* for guidance on running each task. Observe children to identify those who have mastered concepts and those who require further consolidation.

3 Use these Roman numerals to make the following numbers:

I   I   I   I   V

X   X   X   X   L   C

a   31   c   89   e   93

b   54   d   67   f   79

Now work out what these Roman numbers are in our numbers.

g   XVII   i   LXXXIV   k   XLII

h   XXXIX   j   LXIX   l   XCVIII

Did you know?

We still use Roman numerals in many places today.

This medal is from the 1980 Winter Olympic Games. It shows that these were the 13th games since the Winter Olympics began in 1924.

Applying addition and subtraction

Total recording time:

5 hours

Available recording space
Recorded TV

184 GB

Other content
Live TV Pause Buffer

I wonder how many minutes of recording time I have altogether?

Visitors at the aquarium

Number of visitors

1500

1000

500

0

noon   1 p.m.   2 p.m.   3 p.m.   4 p.m.

How many more visitors were there at 2 p.m. than at 1 p.m?

Using mental and written methods to solve problems

Let's learn

There are 100 centimetres in 1 metre so there must be 100 metres in 1 kilometre.

No, there are 1000 metres in a kilometre. Remember, 'kilo' means 'thousand'.

You need:
- Base 10 apparatus
- place-value counters
- clocks

Calculating distances using the written method

A bus stops at 3 stops between 10:50 a.m. and 1:00 p.m. Find the total distance travelled.

Use bars to model the calculation. You know that the distance from Stop A to Stop B is 5428 m and the distance from Stop B to Stop C is 4072 m.

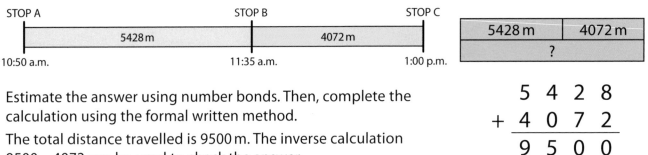

STOP A	STOP B	STOP C
5428 m	4072 m	
10:50 a.m.	11:35 a.m.	1:00 p.m.

5428 m	4072 m
?	

Estimate the answer using number bonds. Then, complete the calculation using the formal written method.

The total distance travelled is 9500 m. The inverse calculation 9500 – 4072 can be used to check the answer.

$$\begin{array}{r} 5\ 4\ 2\ 8 \\ +\ 4\ 0\ 7\ 2 \\ \hline 9\ 5\ 0\ 0 \\ 1\ \ \ 1 \end{array}$$

Calculating durations using mental methods

A number line can help you calculate the total duration of the journey.

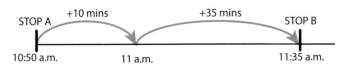

The journey time from Stop A to Stop B is the difference between 10:50 a.m. and 11:35 a.m.

You can show this in steps of 10 minutes + 35 minutes = 45 minutes.

The total duration is the difference between 10:50 a.m. and 1 p.m. You can show this in steps of 10 minutes + 2 hours = 2 hours 10 minutes.

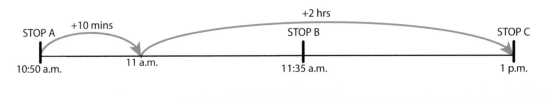

Teacher's Guide

Before working through the *Textbook*, study page 84 of the *Teacher's Guide* to see how the concepts should be introduced. Read and discuss the page with the children. Provide concrete resources to support exploration.

1 Calculate.

Use the bar model to represent each of these calculations. Choose to use a mental or written method to find the answers. Remember to make an estimate first.

a   875 m + 400 m =

b   5463 m – 2372 m =

c   2500 m – 505 m =

d   3582 m + 2714 m =

e   Use the inverse calculations to check your answers.

f   Write the answer to 875 m + 400 m as

           km   m.

2 Calculate.

Find the difference between the pairs of times shown.

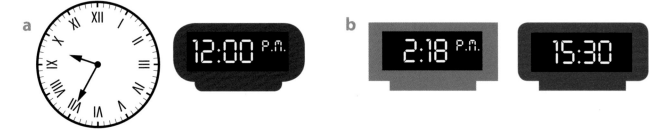

a

b

c   A 24-hour clock shows the time 18:45. What time will it show 120 minutes later?

3 Apply.

Use your class timetable to calculate the duration of different lessons, the morning session or breaks in the day. Here is an example of part of a timetable.

9 a.m.	Registration
9:15 a.m.	English
10:25 a.m.	Break
10:45 a.m.	Maths

4 Think.

The total distance of 2 journeys is 5 km 250 m.

What could the distance of each journey be? Write the distances in metres.

Now find another solution ... and another

How many different solutions can you find? Use a table to organise your solutions.

Teacher's Guide

See page 85 of the *Teacher's Guide* for ideas of how to guide practice. Work through each step together as a class to develop children's conceptual understanding.

71 ★

Bar models and bar charts

Let's learn

The word 'sum' can be used to describe any calculation so 75 + 20 and 95 − 30 are both sums!

You need:
- squared paper
- ruler

No, that's not right. The 'sum' of 2 numbers is the total. It can only be used for addition.

Sums and differences

The unknown value in this bar model is the sum or total of 600 and 450.

Calculate the unknown value with the addition 600 + 450.

A mental method can be used. The number bond 6 + 4 = 10 is related to the bond 600 + 400 = 1000.

You can write the calculation as 600 + 400 + 50 = 1000 + 50 = 1050.

600	450
?	

The unknown value in this bar model is the difference between 1200 and 900.

Calculate the unknown value with the subtraction 1200 − 900. Use a number line, number bonds or related facts to help you.

1200 − 900 is related to the fact 12 − 9 = 3, so 1200 − 900 = 300.

1200	
900	?

Interpreting data

The same values are used in a bar chart of quiz scores.

Team B has 1200 points and Team A has 900 points. 1200 − 900 = 300, so Team B has 300 points more than Team A.

Team C and Team D scored a total of 1050 points between them as 600 + 450 = 1050.

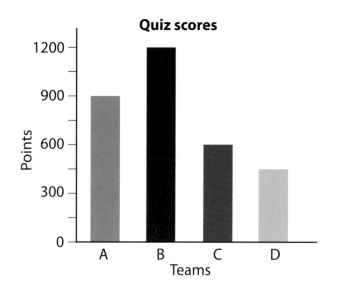

Quiz scores

Teacher's Guide

Before working through the *Textbook*, study page 86 of the *Teacher's Guide* to see how the concepts should be introduced. Read and discuss the page with the children. Provide concrete resources to support exploration.

1

Calculate.

Work out the unknown value each time. Write the calculations that you use to help you.

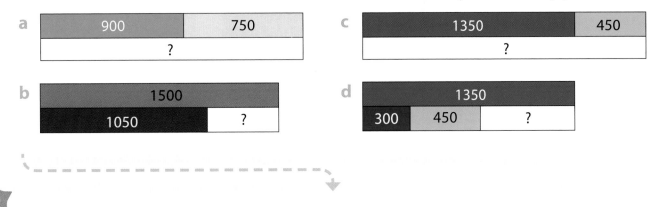

a

900	750
?	

c

1350	450
?	

b

1500	
1050	?

d

1350		
300	450	?

2

Answer these.

Use the bar chart to answer these calculations.

a   How many more points did Team A score than Team D?

b   How many points did Team B and Team C score altogether?

c   Which 2 teams scored a difference of 600 points?

d   How many points were scored in the quiz in total?

3

Draw.

Mia	Tom	Oli	Eva	Ana
750 ml	1500 ml	1050 ml	300 ml	1350 ml

The table shows the amount of water used by each child for their science investigations.

a   Draw a bar chart to show this information. Use the same scale as the Quiz score bar chart.

b   Make up 2 questions to go with the bar chart. Swap your questions with a partner. Answer their questions.

4

Think.

Use the table and bar chart from Step 3 to answer these.

a   Mia and Eva calculated the amount of water they used together. They then compared their total amount of water with the amount used by another child. How many differences can you find?

b   Now pick another 2 children and find the total water used. Compare the total with the amount used by another child. How many differences can you find this time?

Teacher's Guide
See page 87 of the *Teacher's Guide* for ideas of how to guide practice. Work through each step together as a class to develop children's conceptual understanding.

73 ⭐

Solving problems

You need:
- place-value grid
- Base 10 apparatus
- weighing scales

1500 g add 2 kg equals 1502 g.

No, that's not right! 2 kg is 2000 g so the answer to your addition is 3500 g.

Different measures

To calculate with measures you must use the same unit of measurement.

The place-value grid shows how to multiply by 1000 to convert kilograms to grams and multiply by 100 to convert pounds to pence.

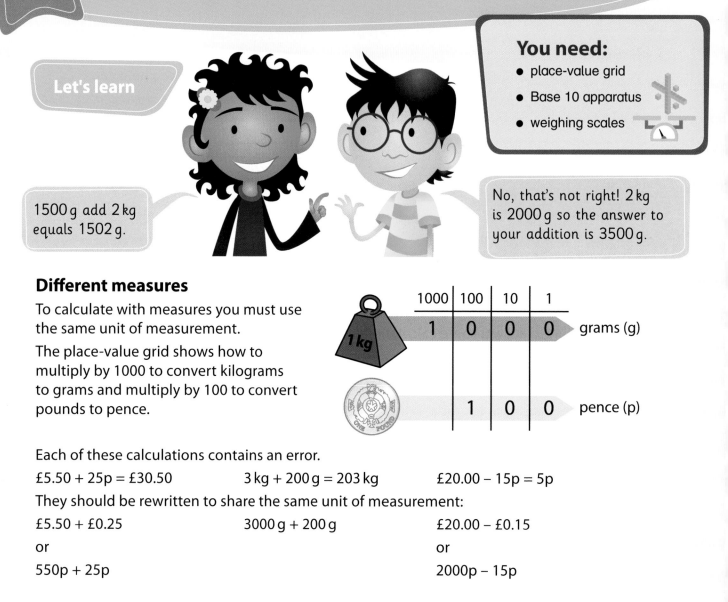

1000	100	10	1	
1	0	0	0	grams (g)
	1	0	0	pence (p)

Each of these calculations contains an error.

£5.50 + 25p = £30.50   3 kg + 200 g = 203 kg   £20.00 – 15p = 5p

They should be rewritten to share the same unit of measurement:

£5.50 + £0.25   3000 g + 200 g   £20.00 – £0.15

or   or

550p + 25p   2000p – 15p

Word problems

Sam buys 850 g of carrots and $2\frac{1}{2}$ kg of potatoes. What is the total mass of vegetables that Sam buys?

500 g is equal to $\frac{1}{2}$ kg. The bars show the equivalence:

The total mass of vegetables can be found using the calculation 2500 g + 850 g.

2500 g + 850 g = 2500 g + 500 g + 350 g
$\qquad\qquad$ = 3000 g + 350 g
$\qquad\qquad$ = 3350 g or 3 kg 350 g

You can use the inverse calculation 3350 g – 850 g to check the answer.

Teacher's Guide

Before working through the *Textbook*, study page 88 of the *Teacher's Guide* to see how the concepts should be introduced. Read and discuss the page with the children. Provide concrete resources to support exploration.

1

Answer these.

Remember to think about the units and make an estimate first.

a   £10.50 + 235p =

c   £12.75 – £4.00 + 50p =

e   99p more than £4.99 =

b   5 kg – 750 g =

d   925 g less than $2\frac{1}{2}$ kg =

Write an inverse calculation to check each of your answers.

2

Calculate.

Use a formal written method to solve these using grams.

a   The mass a plant pot filled with soil is 3 kg 450 g.
Fred plants bulbs that weigh a total of 1362 g. What
is the total mass now?

b   The mass of Mia's cat is 5 kg 929 g. Tom has a
smaller cat. It has a mass of 2385 g. How much
heavier is Mia's cat?

c   Write an inverse calculation to check each of your answers.

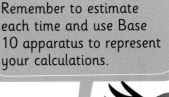

Remember to estimate
each time and use Base
10 apparatus to represent
your calculations.

3

Measure.

Weigh a set of different
items in the classroom.

Record the masses of
each in kilograms and
in grams.

Choose 2 masses at
a time and calculate
their sum and their
difference in grams.

Make up your own word
problems using the masses
for a friend to solve. Draw
a bar model to represent
your problem each time.

4

Think.

Place the different values of money in the grid so the total
of each row is £30 and the total of each column is £20.

£12.45	£11.72	755p
828p	£10.73	927p

Teacher's Guide

See page 89 of the *Teacher's Guide* for ideas of how to guide practice.
Work through each step together as a class to develop children's
conceptual understanding.

75

Time out!

Let's play

Player 1

Teacher's Guide

See pages 90–1 of the *Teacher's Guide*. Explain the rules for each game and allow children to choose which to play. Encourage them to challenge themselves and practise what they have learnt in the unit.

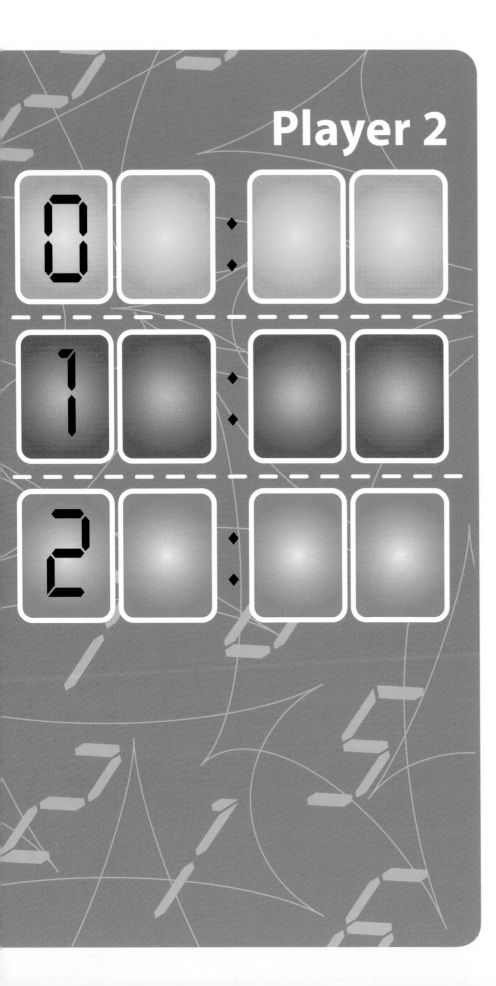

Player 2

You need:

- 2 sets of digit cards 0–9 `0 9`
- pencil and paper clip for the spinner `/`

1 **The early bird …**

The aim of the game is to make three 24-hour times. Think carefully about where you place your digit cards because the player with the earliest times is the winner!

2 **Aim for noon**

The aim of the game is to make three 24-hour times as close to noon as you can. The winner is the player with the closest times.

3 **Your game**

Design your own game. Explain the rules and play with a partner.

And finally …

1

Ana's family are going on holiday. Their flight leaves Glasgow in Scotland at 09:35 and travels 1402 km to Frankfurt, Germany. It then travels another 2435 km to its final destination of Athens in Greece.

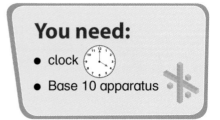

You need:
- clock
- Base 10 apparatus

a   Ana's family arrive at Glasgow airport at 05:50. How long do they have to wait until their flight?

b   Calculate the total distance that the aeroplane flew from Glasgow to Athens.

2

This bar chart shows the amount of money raised by different events for charity.

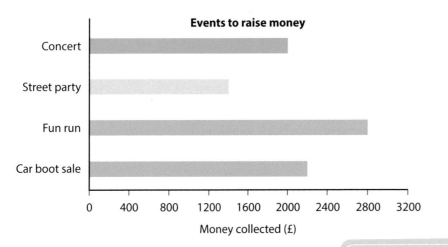

Events to raise money

Money collected (£)

a   Explain whether you agree with Tom.

b   Compare amounts of money raised by:
- the car boot sale and concert
- the fun run and street party
- the street party and car boot sale

c   How much money was raised altogether?

I will use written methods to help me compare the amount of money raised by the different events. Do you agree?

Teacher's Guide

See pages 92–3 of the *Teacher's Guide* for guidance on running each task. Observe children to identify those who have mastered concepts and those who require further consolidation.

★78

3

a   Write each of these masses in order from lightest to heaviest.

b   Calculate the difference between the lightest and heaviest mass.

c   Find some different total masses.

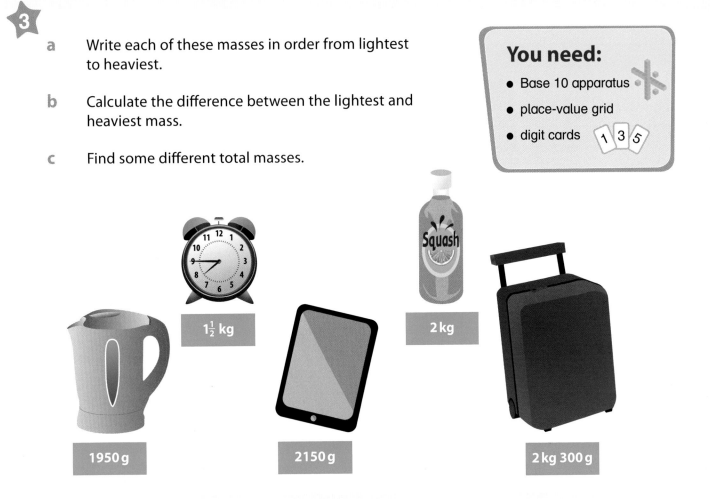

$1\frac{1}{2}$ kg

2 kg

1950 g

2150 g

2 kg 300 g

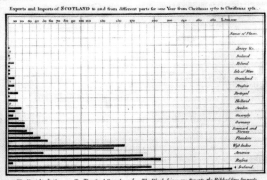

Did you know?

William Playfair was born in Dundee in Scotland on 22 September 1759. He trained as an engineer but he also had many other careers. He is most famous for inventing bar charts and pie charts because he wanted to share information and show people how money was being spent by businesses. These were printed in his famous book called the Commercial and Political Atlas, which was published in 1786.

William Playfair placed his charts in books and newspapers for others to see. People found them so useful that they also began to share information in the same way.

Fractions and decimals

I wonder what fraction this slice of apple is of the whole apple?

If I eat $\frac{3}{10}$ of this chocolate bar, what fraction would be left?

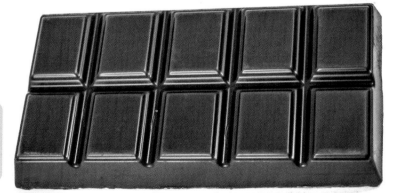

I wonder how many metres wide 1 paving slab is?

If these corn on the cobs were shared equally between 4 people, how much would each person get?

I wonder how much $\frac{1}{10}$ of this money would be?

Teacher's Guide
Look at the pictures with the children and discuss the questions.
See pages 94–5 of the *Teacher's Guide* for key ideas to draw out.

81 ★

Let's learn

$\frac{1}{4}$ can't be the same as $\frac{2}{8}$. They are different numbers.

They are the same! $\frac{1}{4}$ of 8 apples is 2. $\frac{2}{8}$ of 8 apples is also 2. They look different but the value is the same.

You need:
- strips of paper
- ruler
- scissors

Equivalent fractions

These fraction models show that $\frac{1}{4}$, $\frac{2}{8}$ and $\frac{3}{12}$ are equivalent.

How many quarters, eighths and twelfths would be equivalent to $\frac{1}{2}$?

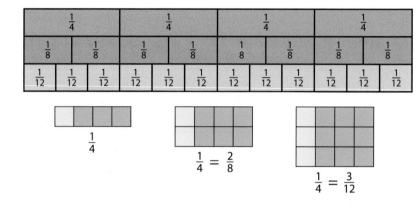

$\frac{1}{4}$

$\frac{1}{4} = \frac{2}{8}$

$\frac{1}{4} = \frac{3}{12}$

These fraction models show that $\frac{1}{3}$, $\frac{2}{6}$ and $\frac{3}{9}$ are equivalent.

How many thirds, sixths and ninths would be equivalent to 1 whole?

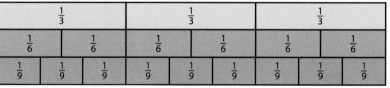

$\frac{1}{3}$

$\frac{1}{3} = \frac{2}{6}$

$\frac{1}{3} = \frac{3}{9}$

Adding and subtracting fractions

It is easy to add and subtract fractions with the same denominator.

The denominators stays the same – just add or subtract the numerator.

Use diagrams or paper strips to explain why these fraction statements are true:

$\frac{5}{8} + \frac{7}{8} = \frac{12}{8} = 1\frac{4}{8} = 1\frac{1}{2}$

$2 - 1\frac{1}{3} = 1 - \frac{1}{3} = \frac{3}{3} - \frac{1}{3} = \frac{2}{3}$

$\frac{1}{4} + \frac{3}{4} = \frac{4}{4} = 1$

$2 - \frac{5}{6} = 1 + 1 - \frac{5}{6} = 1 + \frac{6}{6} - \frac{5}{6} = 1\frac{1}{6}$

Teacher's Guide

Before working through the *Textbook*, study page 96 of the *Teacher's Guide* to see how the concepts should be introduced. Read and discuss the page with the children. Provide concrete resources to support exploration.

1

Write.

Write down 3 equivalent fractions for each of these.

a $\frac{1}{2}$ c $\frac{1}{5}$ e $\frac{1}{10}$ g $\frac{2}{3}$

b $\frac{1}{3}$ d $\frac{1}{8}$ f $\frac{1}{12}$ h $\frac{5}{8}$

Explain how you found these.

What generalisation have you made?

2

Calculate.

Add these fractions.

a $\frac{4}{5} + \frac{3}{5}$ c $\frac{5}{8} + \frac{3}{8} + \frac{7}{8}$

b $\frac{2}{3} + \frac{2}{3}$ d $\frac{1}{4} + \frac{3}{4} + \frac{3}{4}$

> Make sure you change the improper fractions to mixed numbers.

Subtract these fractions.

e $\frac{2}{3} - \frac{1}{3}$ g $\frac{4}{5} - \frac{2}{5}$ i $2 - \frac{3}{5}$ k $3 - 2\frac{1}{3}$

f $\frac{3}{4} - \frac{1}{4}$ h $\frac{5}{6} - \frac{3}{6}$ j $2 - 1\frac{1}{4}$ l $3 - 1\frac{1}{8}$

3

Measure.

Take 3 strips of paper. Measure them so that each is 30 cm long.

Use a ruler to divide your strips into 5ths, 10ths and 15ths.

Label each part with its fraction.

Cut each strip into its fraction parts.

Use the parts to find as many equivalent fractions as you can.

Make a list of them.

4

Think.

Ana added some fractions together. The sum was $2\frac{1}{2}$.

All her fractions had the same denominator.

> Write down some of the possible fractions that I could have added.

Teacher's Guide

See page 97 of the *Teacher's Guide* for ideas of how to guide practice. Work through each step together as a class to develop children's conceptual understanding.

83 ★

Decimals and equivalences

Let's learn

I think 0.2 is the equivalent decimal to $\frac{1}{2}$.

That's not right! 0.2 is equivalent to $\frac{2}{10}$ and $\frac{1}{5}$.

You need:
- Base 10 apparatus
- place-value grids
- digit cards
- coins

Decimals and fraction equivalences

You can make a fraction equivalent to another fraction and a decimal.

Look at the number lines. $\frac{1}{10}$ is equivalent to 0.1, $\frac{2}{10}$ is equivalent to 0.2, and so on.

You can use Base 10 apparatus to make decimal numbers and their fraction equivalences.

$1.8 = 1\frac{8}{10}$

$2.34 = 2\frac{34}{100}$

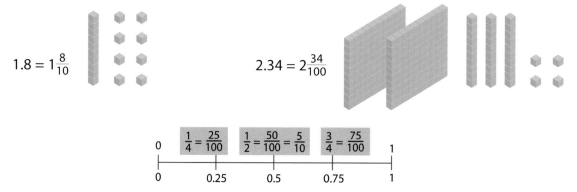

Counting in tenths and hundredths

Counting in tenths and hundredths is just like counting in whole numbers.

Tenths are ones that have been divided by 10.

Hundredths are tenths that have been divided by ten or ones that have been divided by 100.

The first number has been divided by 10 to make the second number. The digits have all moved 1 place to the right.

The first number has been divided by 100 to make the third number. The digits have all moved 2 places to the right.

100	10	1	.	$\frac{1}{10}$	$\frac{1}{100}$
5	9	1			
	5	9	.	1	
		5	.	9	1

Teacher's Guide

Before working through the *Textbook*, study page 98 of the *Teacher's Guide* to see how the concepts should be introduced. Read and discuss the page with the children. Provide concrete resources to support exploration.

1

Write.

Write the decimal equivalents for these fractions.

a $\frac{1}{10}$ d $\frac{1}{2}$ g $\frac{1}{100}$ j $\frac{9}{100}$

b $\frac{3}{10}$ e $\frac{1}{4}$ h $\frac{2}{100}$ k $\frac{12}{100}$

c $\frac{7}{10}$ f $\frac{3}{4}$ i $\frac{6}{100}$ l $\frac{36}{100}$

2

Write.

Write these decimals as fractions.

a   0.2   d   0.8   g   0.75

b   0.5   e   0.12   h   0.45

c   0.9   f   0.25

Simplify any fractions in your answers if you can.

3

Apply.

Make these amounts of money using the fewest coins.

a   £1.30   c   £1.70   e   £2.60

b   £1.10   d   £2.50   f   £3.90

Describe the place value of each amount using the words 'whole number' and 'tenth'.

Divide each amount by 10. Make the quotient using 10p and 1p coins.

Describe the place value of each amount now.

4

Think.

a   Use these digit cards to make a number between 6.2 and 6.82.

b   What is the largest number you can make using all 4 cards?

c   What is the smallest number you can make using all 4 cards?

Teacher's Guide

See page 99 of the *Teacher's Guide* for ideas of how to guide practice. Work through each step together as a class to develop children's conceptual understanding.

85 ★

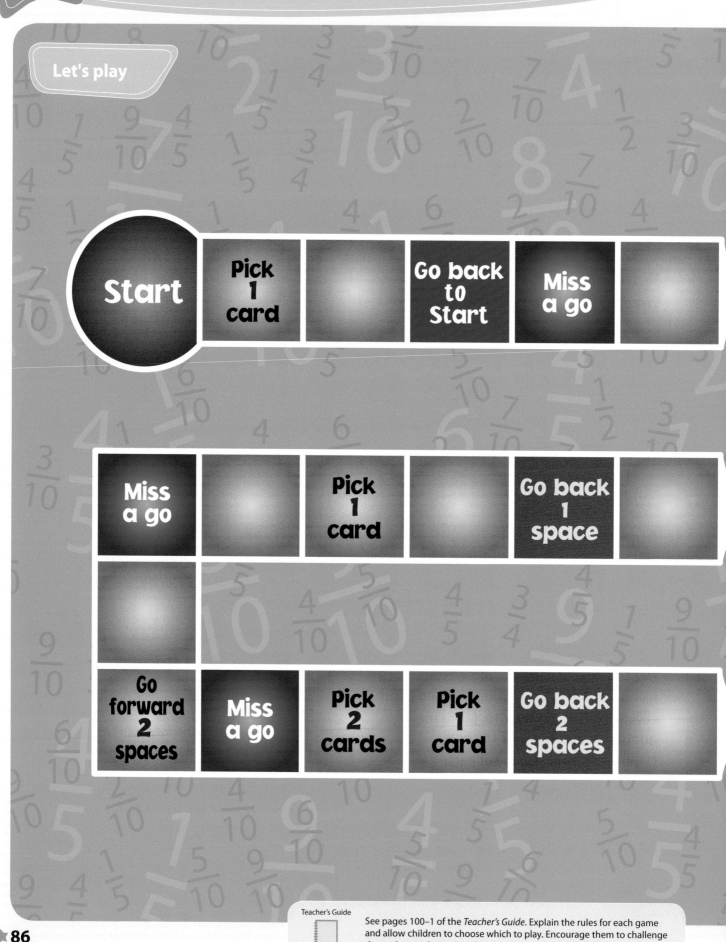

Let's play

Start · Pick 1 card · Go back to Start · Miss a go

Miss a go · Pick 1 card · Go back 1 space

Go forward 2 spaces · Miss a go · Pick 2 cards · Pick 1 card · Go back 2 spaces

Teacher's Guide

See pages 100–1 of the *Teacher's Guide*. Explain the rules for each game and allow children to choose which to play. Encourage them to challenge themselves and practise what they have learnt in the unit.

Pick 2 cards

Pick 2 cards

Pick 1 card

Go forward 2 spaces

Pick 2 cards

Miss a go

Pick 1 card

Pick 2 cards

Pick 1 card

Finish

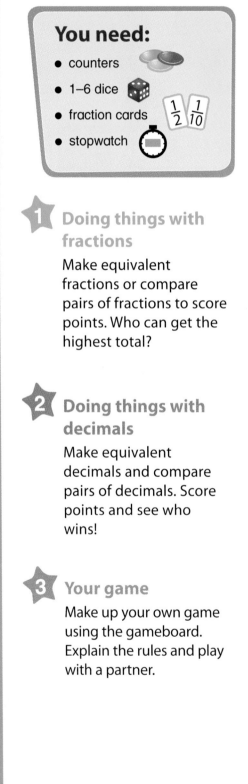

You need:

- counters
- 1–6 dice
- fraction cards
- stopwatch

1 **Doing things with fractions**

Make equivalent fractions or compare pairs of fractions to score points. Who can get the highest total?

2 **Doing things with decimals**

Make equivalent decimals and compare pairs of decimals. Score points and see who wins!

3 **Your game**

Make up your own game using the gameboard. Explain the rules and play with a partner.

And finally …

Let's review

1

Sort these fractions into 4 groups of equivalent fractions.

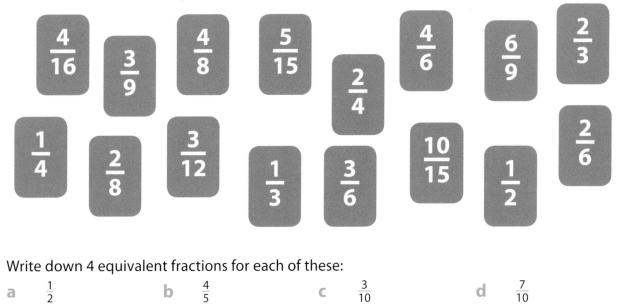

Write down 4 equivalent fractions for each of these:

a $\frac{1}{2}$ b $\frac{4}{5}$ c $\frac{3}{10}$ d $\frac{7}{10}$

Now write down 6 of your own fractions. Find 4 equivalent fractions for each.
Give them to your partner to check.

2

Write and solve for each pair of fractions:
- 1 addition calculation
- 1 subtraction calculation.

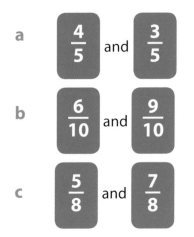

a $\frac{4}{5}$ and $\frac{3}{5}$

b $\frac{6}{10}$ and $\frac{9}{10}$

c $\frac{5}{8}$ and $\frac{7}{8}$

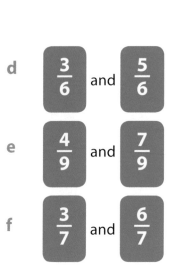

d $\frac{3}{6}$ and $\frac{5}{6}$

e $\frac{4}{9}$ and $\frac{7}{9}$

f $\frac{3}{7}$ and $\frac{6}{7}$

Teacher's Guide — See pages 102–3 of the *Teacher's Guide* for guidance on running each task. Observe children to identify those who have mastered concepts and those who require further consolidation.

3 Copy and complete this number line.

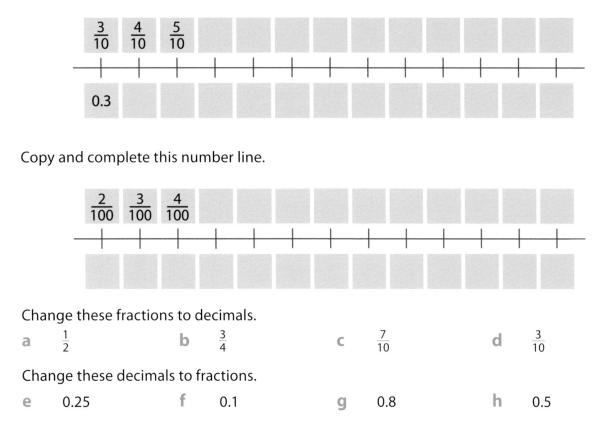

Copy and complete this number line.

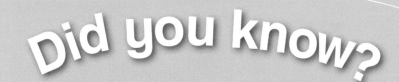

Change these fractions to decimals.

a $\frac{1}{2}$ b $\frac{3}{4}$ c $\frac{7}{10}$ d $\frac{3}{10}$

Change these decimals to fractions.

e 0.25 f 0.1 g 0.8 h 0.5

Did you know?

Lots of people use decimals and fractions in daily life.

Chefs need to understand decimals and fractions so they can measure out ingredients, like 2.5 kg of flour or $\frac{1}{2}$ tablespoon of pepper.

How many drinks are there altogether?

I wonder how many of those I can afford?

How many people will that feed?

Teacher's Guide
Look at the pictures with the children and discuss the questions.
See pages 104–5 of the *Teacher's Guide* for key ideas to draw out.

91 ★

Multiplication table facts

Let's learn

You need:
- bead string
- number rods
- calendar

I know the hardest one in the 7 times table. It is 7 × 8 = 54.

That's not right. 7 × 7 = 49 so adding another 7 makes 56, not 54.

Counting in 7s

Look at the number line. The jumps are in steps of 7.

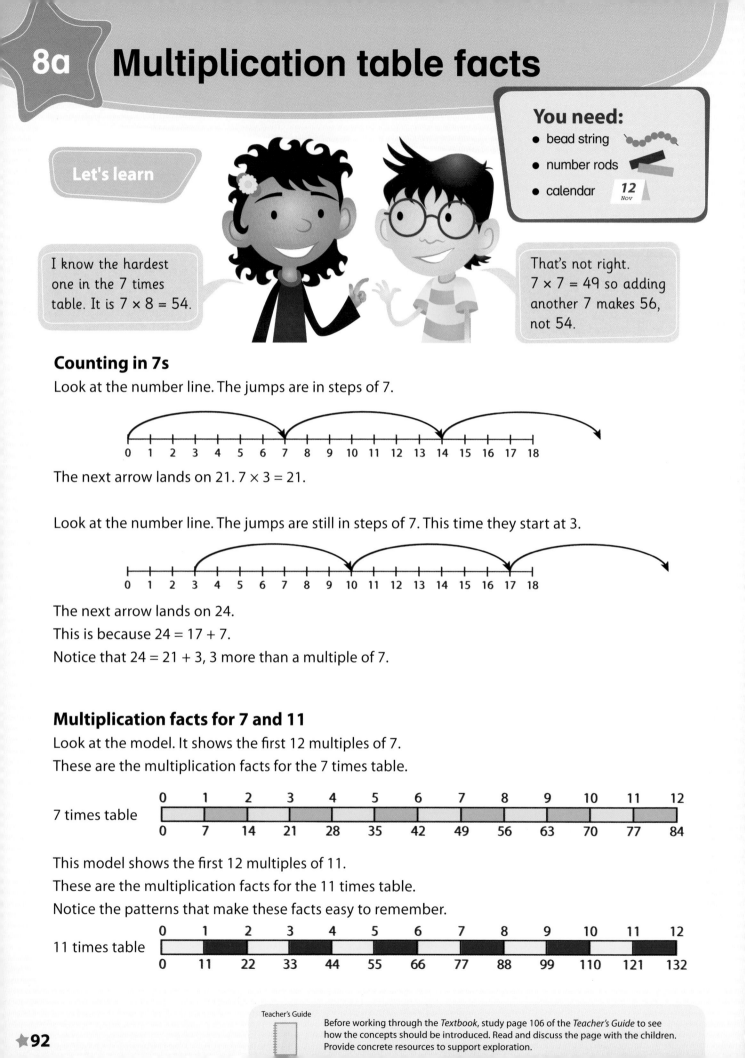

The next arrow lands on 21. 7 × 3 = 21.

Look at the number line. The jumps are still in steps of 7. This time they start at 3.

The next arrow lands on 24.

This is because 24 = 17 + 7.

Notice that 24 = 21 + 3, 3 more than a multiple of 7.

Multiplication facts for 7 and 11

Look at the model. It shows the first 12 multiples of 7.

These are the multiplication facts for the 7 times table.

7 times table	0	1	2	3	4	5	6	7	8	9	10	11	12
	0	7	14	21	28	35	42	49	56	63	70	77	84

This model shows the first 12 multiples of 11.

These are the multiplication facts for the 11 times table.

Notice the patterns that make these facts easy to remember.

11 times table	0	1	2	3	4	5	6	7	8	9	10	11	12
	0	11	22	33	44	55	66	77	88	99	110	121	132

Teacher's Guide

Before working through the *Textbook*, study page 106 of the *Teacher's Guide* to see how the concepts should be introduced. Read and discuss the page with the children. Provide concrete resources to support exploration.

1

Answer these.

a   Count in 7s from 0. Stop when you have passed 50.

b   Count in 7s from 4. Do you land on 40?

c   Count in 7s backwards from 100. Do you land on 30?

d   Count in 7s backwards from 20. What is the first negative number you land on?

e $7 \times 6 =$

f $7 \times 9 =$

g $7 \times 11 =$

h $7 \times 8 =$

2

Answer these.

Copy and complete.

a   4, ▢, 26

b   11, ▢, ▢, ▢, 39

c   52, ▢, ▢, 31, ▢

d   ▢, ▢, 15, 22, ▢

e $84 = 7 \times$ ▢

f $42 \div 7 =$ ▢

g $121 \div 11 =$ ▢

h   ▢ $= 56 \div 7$

3

Solve.

Use your knowledge of multiplication tables to help Tom and Ana solve these calendar problems.

a   It is 6th October. Ana's birthday is in exactly 5 weeks. What date is her birthday?

b   It is 3rd April. Tom's birthday was exactly 3 weeks ago. What date is his birthday?

c   Ana spends 7 hours in school each day. How many hours is that each week?

d   Tom is going on holiday in 6 weeks. How many days is that?

e   How many days is it from 21st August to 2nd November? Give your answer in weeks and days.

4

Think.

a   You can work out 7×11 by working out $7 \times 10 = 70$ and adding $7 \times 1 = 7$. Will this work for other multiplication facts for 11? How do you know?

b   Today is Tuesday. What day of the week will it be in 40 days? Can you find a quick way to work this out? Make up some more problems like this and use your quick way to solve them.

Let's learn

You need:
- counters
- number rods
- 1–6 dice

I know my zero times table.
$7 \times 0 = 7$!

That's not right.
7 lots of nothing is still nothing – so it can't be 7.

Zero and one

Think about what number ⬤ could stand for if 🔺 can be any number.

Notice that multiplying by ⬤ keeps the value of 🔺 the same.

The only number that does that is 1, e.g. $5 \times 1 = 5$

Think about what number 🔺 could stand for if ⬤ can be any number.

Notice that multiplying by 🔺 makes the value of ⬤ the same as 🔺.

The only number that does that is zero, e.g. $0 \times 7 = 0$

Multiplying 3 numbers

Look at $3 \times 7 \times 2$

You can only multiply together 2 numbers at a time.

You can multiply 3 by 7 first, then multiply your answer by 2.

This diagram shows 3×7 which is then multiplied by 2.

You can multiply 7 by 2 first, then multiply 3 by your answer.

This diagram shows 3 lots of 7×2.

In each case the answer is 42 so $3 \times 7 \times 2 = 42$

Teacher's Guide
Before working through the *Textbook*, study page 108 of the *Teacher's Guide* to see how the concepts should be introduced. Read and discuss the page with the children. Provide concrete resources to support exploration.

1

Calculate.

a $7 \times 0 =$ c $0 \times 11 =$ e $2 \times 3 \times 5 =$ g $6 \times 4 \times 2 =$

b $3 \times 1 =$ d $1 \times 8 =$ f $10 \times 2 \times 5 =$ h $7 \times 1 \times 8 =$

2

Answer these.

Copy and complete.

a $8 \times \boxed{} = 8$ d $0 = \boxed{} \div 12$ g $48 \div 6 = 2 \times 2 \times \boxed{}$

b $0 = 11 \times \boxed{}$ e $2 \times \boxed{} \times 7 = 42$ h $8 \times \boxed{} \times \boxed{} = 40$

c $5 \div \boxed{} = 5$ f $28 = 2 \times 2 \times \boxed{}$

3

Solve.

Solve these problems using number rods.

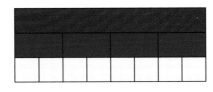

a   The bar model represents the product of 3 single-digit numbers. Write down 4 possible products that it could represent.

b   If each of the white bars represents 2, what do the other bars represent?

c   If each of the red bars represents 6, what do the other bars represent?

d   If the brown bar represents 8, what do the other bars represent?

> Can you make another arrangement of rods with 3 layers so that each layer has the same size of rod? And another?

4

Think.

a   Use the digits 0, 1, 2 and 3 once each to make each of the numbers from 1 to 10. You may use any of the operations $+$, $-$, $\times$ and $\div$ and you may place the digits next to each other to form 2-digit numbers, e.g. $1 = 1 + 2 \times 3 \times 0$.

b   Throw 3 normal dice 10 times. Each time, multiply together the 3 numbers that are thrown and record the result. What do you notice about the products?

Teacher's Guide

See page 109 of the *Teacher's Guide* for ideas of how to guide practice. Work through each step together as a class to develop children's conceptual understanding.

Written methods

Let's learn

4 × 3 = 12
4 × 5 = 20
12 + 20 = 32

I want to buy 4 pens for 35p each. It will cost me 32p.

That's not right! That's less than 1 pen costs. You've multiplied 3 by 4 instead of multiplying 30 by 4.

Writing it out

You can work out multiplications using the column method.

Look at 6 × 23.

100	10	1
	2	3

1 Work out 3 × 6 = 18 first.

Write the tens digit in the tens column below the line.
Write the 8 in the ones column.

2 Then work out 20 × 6 = 120.

Add the extra ten to give 130.

3 The answer is 138.

```
   1              2              3
     23             23             23
  ×   6          ×   6          ×   6
   138            138            138
    1              1              1
```

Solving problems

These 2 bar models show different ways of answering the following problem:

Dog biscuits cost 20p and chewy treats cost 40p.

Tom buys a biscuit and a treat for each of his 3 dogs.

How much does that cost?

| 20 | 40 |
| 20 | 40 | (20 + 40) × 3
| 20 | 40 |

There are 2 steps in the calculation:
- 20 + 40 = 60
- 60 × 3 = 180p

The cost is 180p or £1.80.

| 20 | 20 | 20 | 20 × 3 + 40 × 3
| 40 | 40 | 40 |

This model uses the same bars but they are arranged differently.

There are 3 steps in the calculation:
- 20 × 3 = 60
- 40 × 3 = 120
- 60 + 120 = 180p

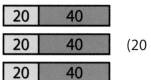
Teacher's Guide

Before working through the *Textbook*, study page 110 of the *Teacher's Guide* to see how the concepts should be introduced. Read and discuss the page with the children. Provide concrete resources to support exploration.

1 Calculate.

a $32 \times 4 =$

b $6 \times 41 =$

c $57 \times 8 =$

d $86 \times 7 =$

e $5 \times 6 + 11 =$

f $4 \times 8 + 6 \times 8 =$

g $3 \times 6 + 7 \times 2 =$

> Remember, always multiply before you add. Draw bar models to help you.

2 Answer these.

Copy and complete.

a
```
    5 ☐
  ×   3
  1 5 6
```

b
```
    4 6
  ×   ☐
  2 7 6
```

c
```
  ☐ ☐
  ×   9
  7 8 3
```

d
```
  ☐ ☐
  ×   3
  3 9 2
```

Remember, always multiply before you add. Draw bar models to help you.

e $6 \times 3 + \boxed{} = 23$

f $42 = 8 \times \boxed{} + 10$

g $63 = 2 \times 9 + \boxed{} \times 9$

h $3 \times 5 + \boxed{} = 7 \times 2 + 9$

3 Solve.

Solve these word problems using multiplication and addition

a   Ana watches 4 cartoons, each lasting 20 minutes, then a film lasting 70 minutes. How long was she watching, in hours and minutes?

b   Tom buys 6 apples at 43p each. How much does that cost altogether?

c   Peaches weigh 100 g each and oranges weigh 120 g each. How much do 7 peaches and 7 oranges weigh altogether?

d   How many days are there in 26 weeks?

e   A piece of cod costs £3.60 and a portion of chips costs £1.80. How much do 4 portions of cod and chips cost?

4 Think.

a   Use 3 of the numbers from 1 to 6 to replace the boxes in $\boxed{}\boxed{} \times \boxed{}$. Which arrangement of numbers gives the highest product?

b   Use 4 of the numbers from 1 to 6 to replace the boxes so that $\boxed{} \times \boxed{} + \boxed{} \times \boxed{} = 24$.

> What if you use 4 of the numbers from 1 to 9? How many ways are there of doing it?

Teacher's Guide

See page 111 of the *Teacher's Guide* for ideas of how to guide practice. Work through each step together as a class to develop children's conceptual understanding.

97

8d Scaling

You need:
- number rods
- weighing scales
- sand
- measuring jug

My teacher is two times as tall as I am. I am 3 feet tall so my teacher is 5 feet tall.

That's not right! Two times as tall as 3 feet is 6 feet. 2 × 3 = 6. You have added 2 instead of multiplying by 2.

Scaling up

Look at the bar model.

The orange bar is 4 times as long as the yellow bar.

It has been scaled up by 4.

The yellow bar could represent 100 which would mean the orange bar represents 400.

The yellow bar could represent 2 which would mean the orange bar represents 8.

400 is 4 times as large as 100.

8 is 4 times as large as 2.

Scaling down

Look at the bar model.

The green bar is 5 times shorter than the yellow bar.

It has been scaled down by 5.

The yellow bar could represent 100 which would mean the green bar represents 20.

The yellow bar could represent 1 which would mean the green bar represents one fifth.

20 is 5 times smaller than 100.

One fifth is 5 times smaller than 1.

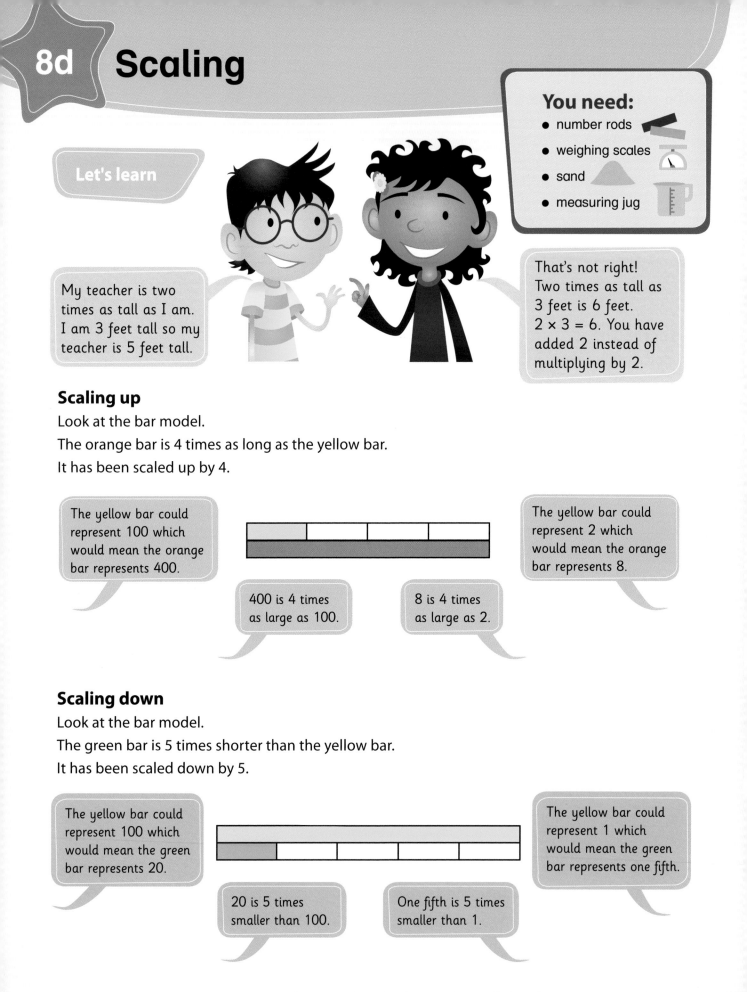

Teacher's Guide

Before working through the *Textbook*, study page 112 of the *Teacher's Guide* to see how the concepts should be introduced. Read and discuss the page with the children. Provide concrete resources to support exploration.

1

Answer these.

Represent each answer using a bar model.

a   What number is 3 times as large as 4?

b   What number is 7 times as large as 2?

c   What number is 6 times as large as 8?

d   What number is 8 times as large as 7?

e   What number is 3 times smaller than 15?

f   What number is 5 times smaller than 35?

g   What number is 10 times smaller than 40?

h   What number is 4 times smaller than 20?

2

Calculate.

Use the bar model to help you answer these questions.

a   How many times as large as 5 is 60?

b   How many times as large as 2 is 40?

c   42 is 6 times the size of a number. What is that number?

d   What number is half the size of 22?

e   7 is one third of the size of a number. What is that number?

f   8 is one tenth of the size of a number. What is that number?

3

Measure.

Pancakes
Serves 8
100 g flour
2 eggs
300 ml milk

a   Measure the flour and milk. Now scale each ingredient up by 3 times. Measure the flour and milk again. How much do you have now?

b   Scale the recipe down by half. How much flour will be needed? How much milk will be needed? How many eggs? Check your answers by measuring.

4

Think.

Look at the diagram.

3 blue bars match 1 red bar.

5 blue bars match 2 green bars.

Choose a pair of coloured rods. How many of each do you need to make matching lengths? Is there more than 1 answer?

Repeat with a second pair of rods. What do you notice?

Teacher's Guide

See page 113 of the *Teacher's Guide* for ideas of how to guide practice. Work through each step together as a class to develop children's conceptual understanding.

99

Lucky numbers

Let's play

Teacher's Guide See pages 114–15 of the *Teacher's Guide*. Explain the rules for each game and allow children to choose which to play. Encourage them to challenge themselves and practise what they have learnt in the unit.

Game 1

- Score 3 for a multiple of 7
- Score 3 for a multiple of 11
- Score 2 for a multiple of 6
- Score 2 for a multiple of 9

Game 2

- Score 3 for making 1 or 0
- Score a bonus point if you use all 3 numbers
- Score a bonus point if you use multiplication
- Score 2 bonus points if you use division

You need:

- 1–6 dice (3)
- whiteboard and pens

1 **Making multiples**

Use the dice numbers to make a multiple of 6, 7, 9 or 11.

2 **Making nothing or one**

Use the dice numbers to make 0 or 1.

3 **Your game**

Make up your own game using the gameboard.

And finally …

1

Tom has got all his homework questions wrong.

Work out the correct answers.

Now write some feedback to explain to Tom where he went wrong.

a $1 \times 0 = $ ___1___

b
$$\begin{array}{r} 67 \\ \times \quad 8 \\ \hline 486 \end{array}$$

c What number is 3 times as large as 4? ___7___

d $2 \times 5 \times 7 = $ ___140___

e $11 \times 11 = $ ___111___

f What number is 6 times smaller than 24? ___18___

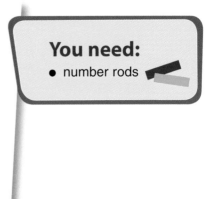

You need:
- number rods

2

This is the multiplication table for 7.

Each letter stands for one of the digits 0 to 9.

The multiplication table facts are not in the correct order.

Work out which digit each letter stands for.

$HH \times F = FF$

$G \times F = HD$

$HC \times F = FC$

$J \times F = GH$

$HG \times F = AD$

$D \times F = GA$

$E \times F = DG$

$H \times F = F$

$B \times F = EJ$

$F \times F = DB$

$A \times F = KE$

$K \times F = JK$

You need:
- whiteboard
- pens

Teacher's Guide

See pages 116–17 of the *Teacher's Guide* for guidance on running each task. Observe children to identify those who have mastered concepts and those who require further consolidation.

★102

I chose 3 numbers that add up to 12
$1 + 1 + 10 = 12$.
Their product is
$1 \times 1 \times 10 = 10$

Can you find 3 numbers that add up to 12 with a larger product than Ana's?

Which 3 numbers give the largest value for the product?

Now choose 3 numbers that add up to 10.

Which group of 3 has the largest product?

Can you find a general rule for finding the group of 3 with the largest product?

Test your rule with some other totals.

Did you know?

Seven is a very special number. It is thought to be a lucky number. When people are asked to name a number between 1 and 10 they choose 7 more often than any other number. The number of days in a week is 7 and the Bible states that God made the world in 7 days, resting on the 7th day. There are 7 deadly sins and 7 virtues. People talk about being 'in seventh heaven' when they are very happy. Breaking a mirror is supposed to bring 7 years of bad luck.

Look up the riddle about meeting a man with 7 wives 'as I was going to St Ives'.

Polygons and coordinates

What 2-D shapes can you see?

I wonder how many different combinations of shapes there are?

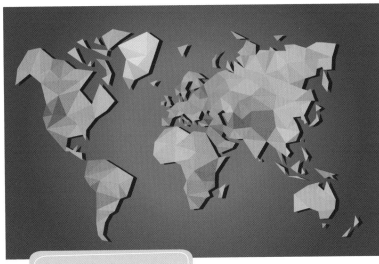

I wonder if you can use polygons to make a picture of *anything*?

I wonder how you can plant an orchard to look so perfect?

How could you describe the position of a chess piece on the board?

Teacher's Guide
Look at the pictures with the children and discuss the questions.
See pages 118–19 of the *Teacher's Guide* for key ideas to draw out.

105

Trapeziums and kites

You need:
- 2-D shapes
- geoboard
- elastic bands
- squared paper
- ruler
- scissors

Let's learn

A trapezium has a pair of parallel lines so it can't have any right angles.

A trapezium must have a pair of parallel sides, but it may also have right angles. Not all trapeziums have right angles though.

All about trapeziums

A trapezium is a quadrilateral with 1 pair of parallel opposite sides.

In an **isosceles trapezium** the sides that are not parallel are equal in length.

This trapezium has line symmetry.

It is also possible to draw a trapezium with **2 right angles.**

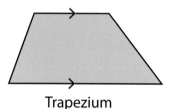

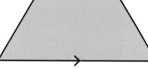

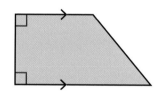

Trapezium   Isosceles trapezium   Trapezium with 2 right angles

All about kites

A kite is a quadrilateral with 2 pairs of sides of equal length.

Each pair of equal sides is next to each other.

When 1 end of the kite has **an angle that is more than 180°** it becomes a dart shape. It is still a kite.

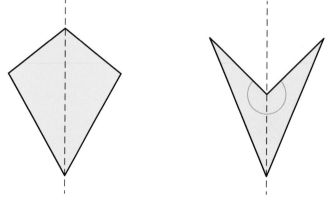

Teacher's Guide

Before working through the *Textbook*, study page 120 of the *Teacher's Guide* to see how the concepts should be introduced. Read and discuss the page with the children. Provide concrete resources to support exploration.

1

Answer these.

Which shapes:

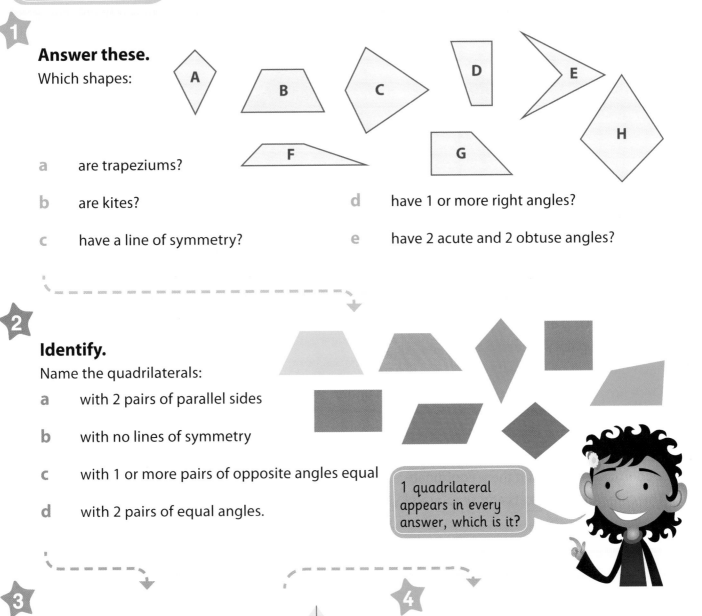

a are trapeziums?

b are kites?

c have a line of symmetry?

d have 1 or more right angles?

e have 2 acute and 2 obtuse angles?

2

Identify.

Name the quadrilaterals:

a with 2 pairs of parallel sides

b with no lines of symmetry

c with 1 or more pairs of opposite angles equal

d with 2 pairs of equal angles.

1 quadrilateral appears in every answer, which is it?

3

Design.

Design 2 different kites.
Draw them on squared paper.

Add diagonal lines.
What do you notice?

Draw another kite.
What do you notice?

What about the diagonals of an inverted kite? (You will need to extend the diagonals.)

Explain the properties of the diagonals of a kite.

4

Investigate.

Make 4 small identical isosceles right-angled triangles.

Investigate how many different polygons you can make using all 4 triangles.

You can only join them:

• matching whole sides

• long side to long side

• short side to short side.

Draw the shapes you make on squared paper. Name them.

Teacher's Guide

See page 121 of the *Teacher's Guide* for ideas of how to guide practice. Work through each step together as a class to develop children's conceptual understanding.

107 ★

Coordinates and translations

Let's learn

I can't remember which axis is the horizontal one – is it x or y?

The x-coordinate is the horizontal one. Think to yourself x is a cross and the x-axis goes a**cross** the page.

Coordinate pairs

Coordinate pairs pinpoint a position on a grid.

Each direction has an axis to use as a measure.

Point (2, 3) is 2 units across in the x direction and 3 units up in the y direction.

Coordinate pairs are always written with the x-coordinate first, then the y-coordinate.

They are put in brackets and separated by a comma.

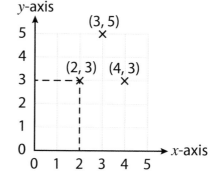

Translating polygons

To translate a shape every point of the shape moves the same distance in the same direction.

Here the shape is moved 3 places right and 4 places up.

Each x-coordinate increases by 3.

Each y-coordinate increases by 4.

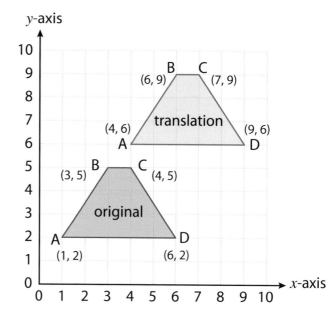

Teacher's Guide

Before working through the *Textbook*, study page 122 of the *Teacher's Guide* to see how the concepts should be introduced. Read and discuss the page with the children. Provide concrete resources to support exploration.

1 Plot.

Draw a 0–10 coordinate grid.
Plot these coordinates.

a   (1, 2), (3, 2), (5, 5), (3, 5)

b   (3, 6), (5, 7), (5, 9), (3, 10), (1, 9), (1, 7)

c   (8, 1), (10, 6), (8, 9), (6, 6)

Join up the points and identify the shapes.

2 Design.

Draw a 0-10 coordinate grid.

a   Plot the coordinates (6, 2), (8, 1), (8, 3).
     Translate the shape 5 squares left.

b   Plot the coordinates
     (0, 4), (1, 7), (3, 7), (2, 4).
     Translate the shape 6 squares right
     and 2 squares up.

Write the new coordinates
after the translation.

Can you explain what has happened to the x- and y-coordinates?

3 Apply.

Here is a code using coordinates.

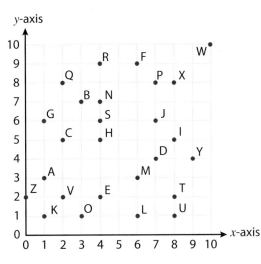

Use the code to answer these questions.

a   (10, 10), (4, 5), (1, 3), (8, 2)
     (8, 5), (4, 6)
     (9, 4), (3, 1), (8, 1), (4, 9)
     (4, 7), (1, 3), (6, 3), (4, 2)?

b   (4, 5), (3, 1), (10, 10)
     (3, 1), (6, 1), (7, 4)
     (1, 3), (4, 9), (4, 2)
     (9, 4), (3, 1), (8, 1)?

c   Now write a question of your own.

4 Investigate.

Draw a 0–10 coordinate grid.

Plot a kite or a trapezium with all coordinate values less than 5.

Investigate what happens when you:

a   double the x-coordinate value of each point

b   double the y-coordinate value of each point

c   double both coordinate values of each point.

Teacher's Guide

See page 123 of the *Teacher's Guide* for ideas of how to guide practice. Work through each step together as a class to develop children's conceptual understanding.

109

Quadrilateral quest

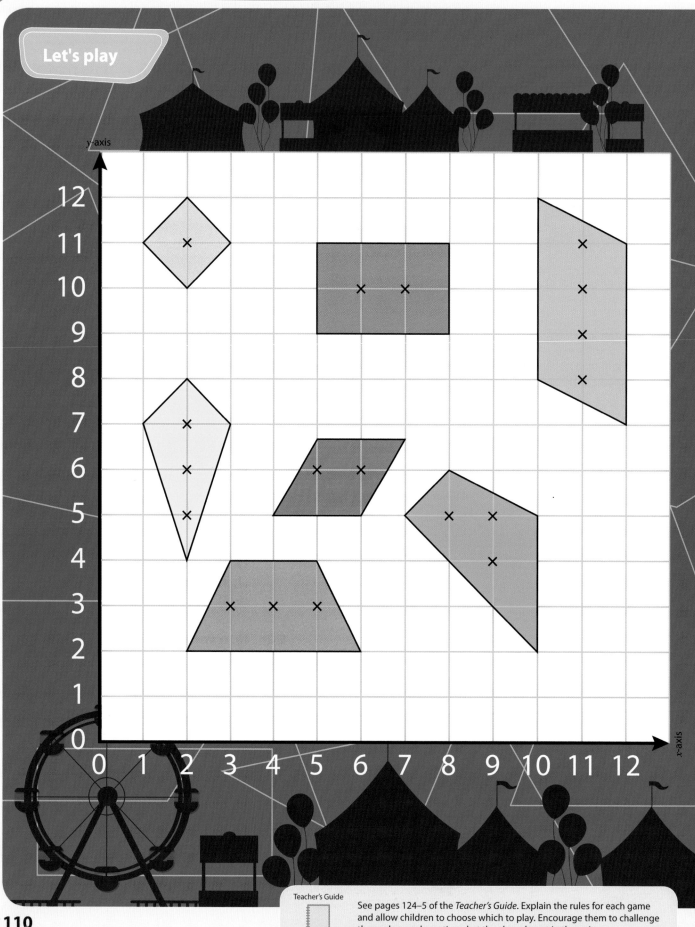

Teacher's Guide

See pages 124–5 of the *Teacher's Guide*. Explain the rules for each game and allow children to choose which to play. Encourage them to challenge themselves and practise what they have learnt in the unit.

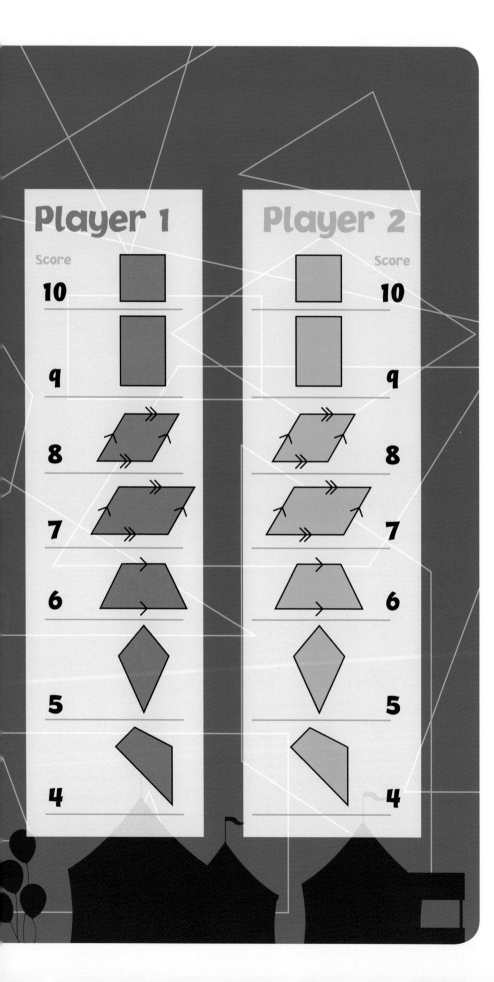

You need:

- 1–12 dice
- counters

1 **Quadrilateral collection**

Locate coordinates and collect all 7 quadrilaterals.

2 **Quadrilateral points**

Generate coordinates and collect points by hitting the quadrilaterals!

3 **Your game**

Make up your own game using the gameboard. Explain the rules and play with a partner.

And finally ...

1

Name these quadrilaterals.

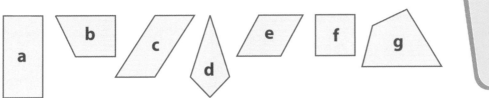

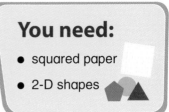

You need:

- squared paper
- 2-D shapes

Look at the table below. All but 1 of the headings are missing.

Fill in the names of the quadrilaterals. Put the row headings in the right places.

| 1 or more pairs of opposite sides parallel | Opposite sides equal | 1 or more pairs of perpendicular sides | 1 or more pairs of sides that are next to each other are equal |

Property	Names of quadrilaterals						
	✔	✘	✔	✘	✔	✔	✘
1 or more lines of symmetry	✔	✘	✘	✔	✔	✔	✘
	✔	✔	✔	✘	✔	✔	✘
	✘	✘	✘	✔	✔	✔	✘
	✔	✔	✘	✘	✘	✔	✘

Key: ✔ means Yes
     ✘ means No

Teacher's Guide

See pages 126–7 of the *Teacher's Guide* for guidance on running each task.
Observe children to identify those who have mastered concepts and those who
require further consolidation.

2

Draw a 0–12 coordinate grid. Plot these coordinates:
(0, 1), (6, 1), (1, 5), (4, 5).

Translate the shape 1 square right and 1 square up.
Colour in the overlap.

Translate the new shape 2 squares right and 2 squares up.
Colour in the overlap.

Translate the new shape 3 squares right and 3 squares up.
Colour in the overlap.

Describe what you notice about the overlap shapes.

You need:
- squared paper
- coloured pencils

3

Here are the coordinates for a kite: (4, 0), (6, 4), (4, 5), (2, 4).

Write new coordinates for the following translations:

- 4 places right
- 5 places up
- 4 places right and 5 places up.

Plot the original and the 3 translations on a
0–10 coordinate grid. Colour them in.

What do you notice about the gap produced in the design?

Try some other quadrilaterals (like a trapezium or an irregular
quadrilateral). Does this happen every time?

You need:
- squared paper
- coloured pencils

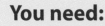

Did you know?

Look at the clever translations
in this cartoon. The translated
octopuses that are the right
way up leave spaces that
make another set of upside-
down octopuses.

Here's another
pattern. Look at these
comic dinosaurs. They
are fun!

Number and place value in real life

I wonder how much this baby weighs in grams?

Kirkenes

Helsinki   1154 km

Roma   5102 km

Oslo   2502 km

Bergen   2626 km

If someone lives 1000 km from Kirkenes, how far would they have to travel to go to Kirkenes then Helsinki?

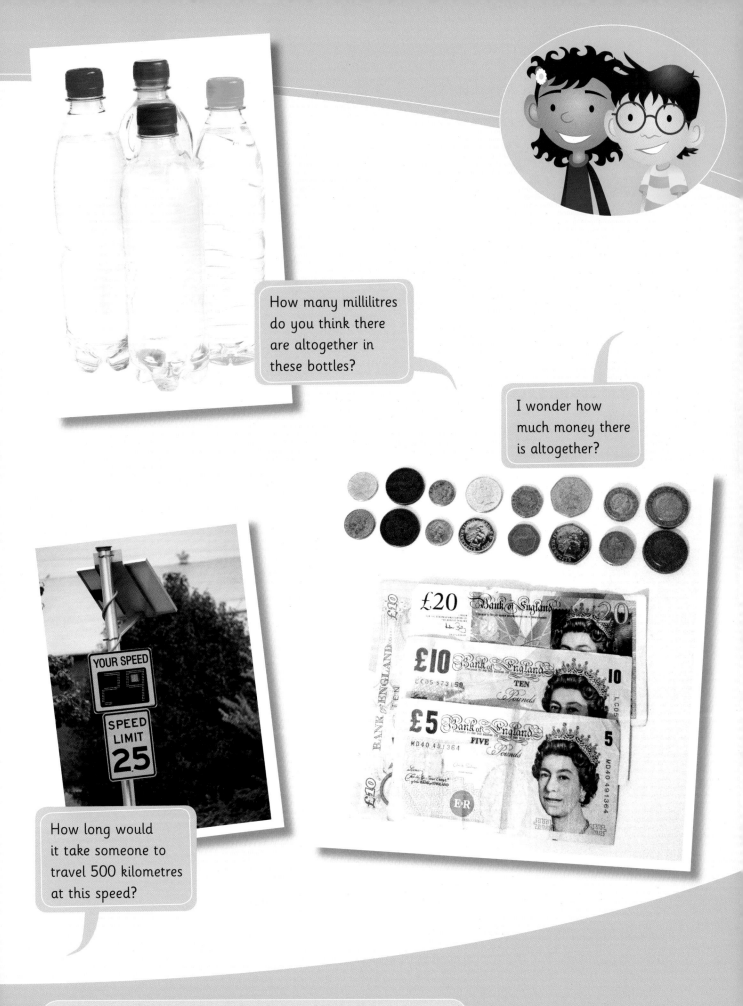

How many millilitres do you think there are altogether in these bottles?

I wonder how much money there is altogether?

How long would it take someone to travel 500 kilometres at this speed?

Teacher's Guide

Look at the pictures with the children and discuss the questions.
See pages 128–9 of the *Teacher's Guide* for key ideas to draw out.

115

25s and 1000s

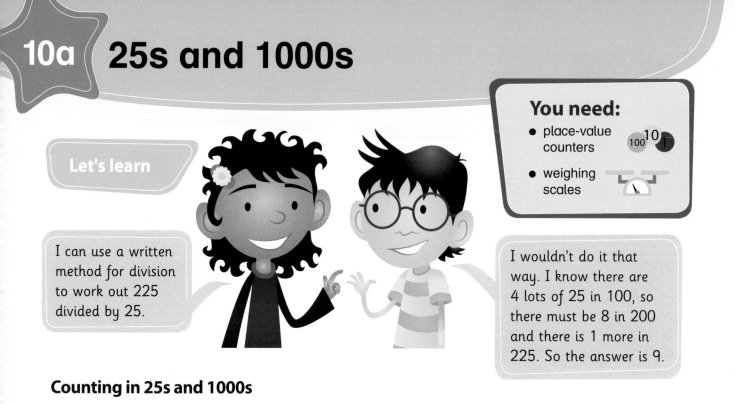

You need:
- place-value counters
- weighing scales

Let's learn

I can use a written method for division to work out 225 divided by 25.

I wouldn't do it that way. I know there are 4 lots of 25 in 100, so there must be 8 in 200 and there is 1 more in 225. So the answer is 9.

Counting in 25s and 1000s

100				200				300			
25	50	75	100	125	150	175	200	225	250	275	300

The bar model shows the first 12 multiples of 25.

There are 4 lots of 25 in 100. The tens and ones digits repeat:

25, 50, 75, 100, 125, 150, 175, 200, 225, 250, 275, 300

You can use the fact that there are 4 lots of 25 in 100 to work out other facts.

1000 is 10×100, so there are $10 \times 4 = 40$ lots of 25 in 1000.

Counting in steps of 1000 is easy.

This number line shows the first 10 multiples of 1000.

```
 |----|----|----|----|----|----|----|----|----|----|
 0   1000 2000 3000 4000 5000 6000 7000 8000 9000 10 000
```

1000 more or less

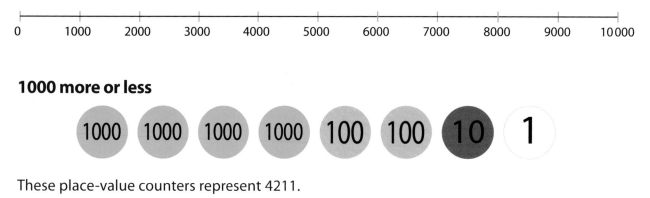

These place-value counters represent 4211.

Imagine adding another green counter. 1000 more than 4211 is 5211.

Imagine taking away 1 of the green counters. 1000 less than 4211 is 3211.

Teacher's Guide

Before working through the *Textbook*, study page 130 of the *Teacher's Guide* to see how the concepts should be introduced. Read and discuss the page with the children. Provide concrete resources to support exploration.

1

Now write down 8 other numbers you might say if you were counting in steps of 25.

Count.

Work out how many lots of 25 there are in each of these numbers.

a   50   c   175   e   275   g   350

b   100   d   225   f   300   h   425

2

Calculate.

Write down the number that is 1000 more than each of these numbers.

a   2354   b   4725   c   7109   d   10 500   e   12 678   f   16 254

What has stayed the same in your numbers? What has changed?

Write down the number that is 1000 less than each of these numbers.

g   5140   h   4209   i   8034   j   10 384   k   14 238   l   16 278

What has stayed the same in your numbers? What has changed?

3

Measure.

Find an item from around the classroom that weighs more than 1 kilogram.

Weigh it on a set of scales. Write down its mass in grams.

a   What would it weigh if it was:
   • 1000 g more?
   • 2000 g more?
   • 3000 g more?

b   What would it weigh if it was 1000 g less?

Do this another 4 times.

4

Think.

At a school fair, children buy tokens to spend on the stalls. Each token is worth 25p.

Ana buys 10 tokens.

She want to have at least 1 go at all 3 stalls.

a   How many different ways can she spend her tokens?

b   For each different way, what is the value of the tokens she spends at each stall?

Teacher's Guide   See page 131 of the *Teacher's Guide* for ideas of how to guide practice. Work through each step together as a class to develop children's conceptual understanding.

117

Place value and measures

Let's learn

£12 and 5 pence is equivalent to 125p.

125p is equivalent to £1.25. £12 and 5 pence is £12.05. The 5 pence are 5 hundredths of a pound. You need to put a zero in the tenths position.

1000s and measures

1	.	10th	100th	1000th
1	.	7	5	(0)

1000	100	10	1
1	7	5	0

The jug contains 1.75 litres.
There are 1000 millilitres in a litre.
0.75 l is 750 ml.
So 1.75 l is equivalent to 1750 ml.

10	1	.	10th	100th
3	1	.	5	6

1000	100	10	1
3	1	5	6

There are 100 pence in a pound.
So £31.56 is equivalent to 3156p.
1000p is equivalent to £10.00.

Place value and time

Our system of telling the time is not Base 10. It is Base 60.

There are 60 minutes in an hour.

On the number line there are 4 divisions every hour. So each represents 60 ÷ 4 = 15 minutes.

Describe the place value of each amount to your partner.

1

Convert.

Convert these amounts to pounds and pence. Record your answers in place-value grids.

10	1	.	10th	100th
		.		

a   245p   b   789p   c   1675p   d   5354p   e   9063p

Convert these litres to millilitres.

f   6 l   g   7.5 l   h   9.5 l   i   3.25 l   j   4.75 l

Convert these grams to kilograms.

k   3000 g   l   4500 g   m   8500 g   n   7250 g   o   9750 g

2

Draw.

Draw time number lines to find the differences between these times.

a   03:55 and 05:45   c   10:50 and 13:10   e   13:51 and 16:06   g   16:08 and 21:25

b   04:35 and 06:20   d   12:25 and 15:50   f   14:54 and 17:32

3

Apply.

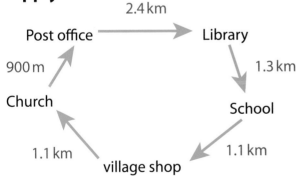

Ollie walks from the post office to the library, then to the school, village shop and church and then back to the post office.

How far has he walked?

Write your answer in 3 different ways; kilometres and metres, metres, kilometres.

4

Think.

What would our number system look like if we worked in Base 5? Our place-value grids might look like this:

125	25	5	1
1	2	3	1

The digits in the grid represent
125 + 50 + 15 + 1 = 191.

Draw your own place-value grid for Base 5 like this. Write a digit in each position. You can only use the digits 0–4. What number do you have?

Do this again… and again… and again.

Teacher's Guide

See page 133 of the *Teacher's Guide* for ideas of how to guide practice. Work through each step together as a class to develop children's conceptual understanding.

119

Number crunch!

Start | 1200 | Throw again | 1350 | 2675 | 1890

Miss a go | 6005 | Go back 3 spaces | 4245 | Miss a go | Throw again

Throw again

5275 | Go back 2 spaces | 4620 | Go back 6 spaces | 6124 | 5908

Teacher's Guide

See pages 134–5 of the *Teacher's Guide*. Explain the rules for each game and allow children to choose which to play. Encourage them to challenge themselves and practise what they have learnt in the unit.

Miss a go

2425

2215

Go back 3 spaces

1905

3635

3050

Throw again

2350

Miss a go

7309

8450

Finish

1 Counting in 1000s

Count in multiples of 1000 for a minute. Who can get the highest score?

2 Pounds and pence

Convert the pence to pounds and pence. The player with the most pounds at the end wins!

3 Your game

Make up your own game using the gameboard. Explain the rules and play with a partner.

Let's review

1

Convert these kilograms to grams. Choose the correct option in each case.

a	5 kg	**5000 g**	50 g	500 g	e	10.75 kg	**10 750 g**	1075 g	107.5 g
b	7 kg	700 g	**7000 g**	70 g	f	12.2 kg	122 000 g	1220 g	**12 200 g**
c	6.5 kg	65 000 g	65 g	**6500 g**	g	16.7 kg	167 g	1670 g	**16 700 g**
d	8.25 kg	8025 g	**8250 g**	825 g	h	20.1 kg	**20 100 g**	2010 g	201 g

For each answer write down 4000 grams more and 4000 grams less.

2

The pictogram shows the favourite animals of the people in a village.

a Write down how many people like each animal.

b How many more people voted for dogs than horses?

c How many more people voted for cats than fish?

d How many people voted altogether?

Make up some questions of your own. You must be able to answer them using the information on the pictogram.

Dog 🐕 🐕 🐕 🐕 🐕

Cat 🐈 🐈 🐈 🐈 🐈 🐈 🐈

Horse 🐎 🐎 🐎

Fish 🐟 🐟 🐟

Each symbol represents 25 people.

Teacher's Guide

See pages 136–7 of the *Teacher's Guide* for guidance on running each task. Observe children to identify those who have mastered concepts and those who require further consolidation.

3

Convert these amounts to pounds and pence.

a 135p

b 863p

c 301p

d 1420p

e 2155p

f 1737p

Use your knowledge of place value to help you.

Order your new amounts from least to greatest.
Round the amounts to the nearest pound.

Use Base 60 to find the differences in these times.

g 07:25 and 08.35

h 09:30 and 12:40

i 11:25 and 13:05

j 14:36 and 16:04

k 18:07 and 19:04

l 20:26 and 23:55

Draw time number lines to help you.

Order the time differences from shortest to longest.

Did you know?

The Babylonians divided the day into 24 hours, each hour into 60 minutes, and each minute to 60 seconds. This is the basis of our time system.

They used a Base 60 number system, rather than the Base 10 system we use today. They used place-value columns like us, but the numbers 1–59 went in the first column. The second column was for numbers from 60 to 60 lots of 60, or 3600! This tables shows some numbers written using the Babylonian system.

3600s	60s	1s	Value
		ᵞᵞ	1 + 1 = 2
		‹ᵞ	10 + 1 = 11
		‹‹	10 + 10 = 20
	ᵞ	ᵞᵞᵞᵞ	60 + 1 + 1 + 1 + 1 = 64
	ᵞᵞᵞ	ᵞᵞ	60 + 60 + 60 + 1 + 1 = 182
ᵞ	ᵞ	‹ᵞ	3600 + 60 + 10 + 1 = 3671
ᵞᵞ	ᵞ		3600 + 3600 + 60 = 7260

Addition and subtraction problems

£4795

£47.95

I can't believe that the coffee maker costs the same as the car! What do you think?

I wonder how far it is from the west coast of Africa to the east coast?

NORTH AMERICA

EUROPE

ASIA

AFRICA

SOUTH AMERICA

AUSTRALIA

ANTARCTICA

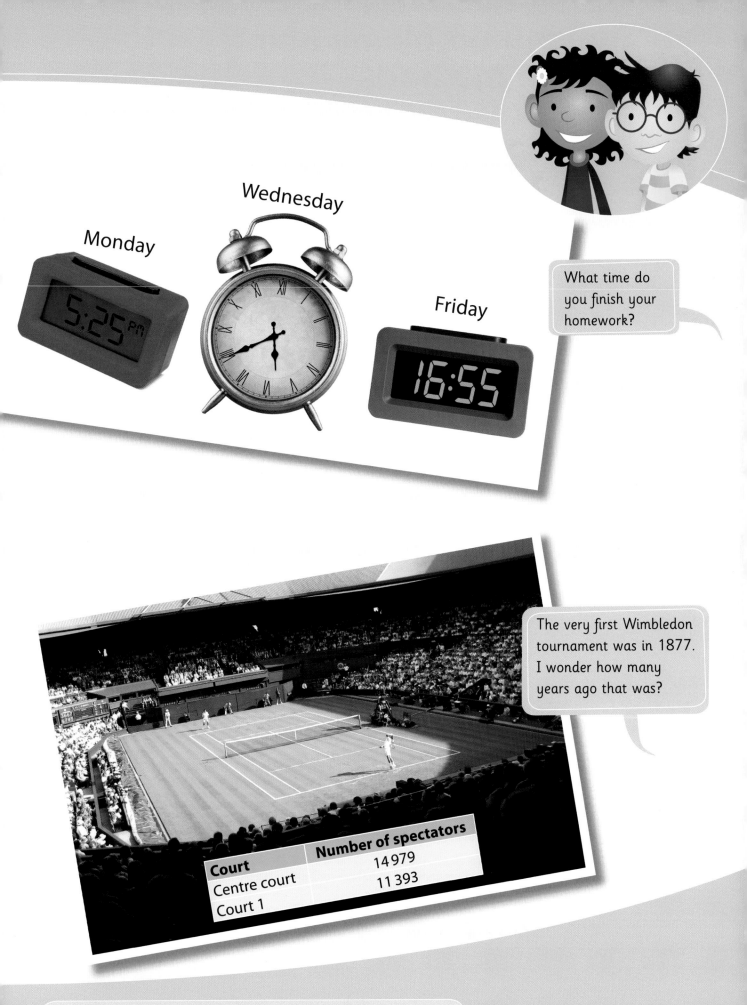

Monday

Wednesday

Friday

5:25 PM

16:55

What time do you finish your homework?

The very first Wimbledon tournament was in 1877. I wonder how many years ago that was?

Court	Number of spectators
Centre court	14 979
Court 1	11 393

Teacher's Guide

Look at the pictures with the children and discuss the questions.
See pages 138–9 of the *Teacher's Guide* for key ideas to draw out.

125

Solving problems using written methods

Let's learn

£1.25 + 50p is equal to £51.25

No, that's not right! 50p is the same as £0.50 not £50. The answer is £1.75.

You need:
- coins 5p 1p 10p
- Base 10 apparatus
- place-value grid
- digit cards 1 3 5

Adding money using a written method

When you calculate with money, make sure the amounts are in the same unit.

To add £1.25 and 50p, first write 50p in pounds or write £1.25 in pence.

£1 is the whole.

50p is $\frac{50}{100}$, or $\frac{5}{10}$, of the whole.

You can write 50p as £0.50.

The zero in the hundredths column is a place holder.

Now you can add £1.25 and £0.50 using a mental method.

(one pound coin)	(ten pence coin)	(one penny coin)
0 .	$\frac{1}{10}$	$\frac{1}{100}$
0 .	5	0

Use a written calculation to add trickier amounts.

To work out £3.68 + 156p, you can do:

368p + 156p or £3.68 + £1.56

```
      p
    3 6 8
  + 1 5 6
    5 2 4
    1   1
```

```
      £
    3 . 6 8
  + 1 . 5 6
    5 . 2 4
    1     1
```

Subtracting money using a written method

You can use a subtraction calculation to check the addition is correct:

524p – 156p or £5.24 – £1.56

```
    ⁴5 ¹¹2 ¹4
  -  1  5 6
     3  6 8
```

```
      £
    ⁴5 . ¹¹2 ¹4
  -  1 .  5 6
     3 .  6 8
```

The answer is the augend you began with so the addition is correct.

Teacher's Guide

Before working through the *Textbook*, study page 140 of the *Teacher's Guide* to see how the concepts should be introduced. Read and discuss the page with the children. Provide concrete resources to support exploration.

Remember to make an estimate first.

1 Calculate.

Use coins to make the following amounts:

a   £1.22   b   £1.45   c   £2.72   d   £3.07

Add £2.35 to each amount.

Write the calculations you use.

Check your answers using the inverse subtraction.

2 Calculate.

Copy and complete these calculations. Use Base 10 apparatus.

Make an estimate first. Check your answers using the inverse calculation.

a
```
  £
  3 . 4 7
+ 1 . 3 6
_____
```

b
```
  £
  4 . 7 2
- 1 . 4 9
_____
```

c
```
  £
  1 5 . 2 8
- 1 2 . 6 4
_____
```

Answer these calculations using the formal written method.

d   £4.17 + 164p   e   635p – £2.62

3 Solve.

a   Ana saves £2.35 each week for 3 weeks. How much more money will she need to buy a game costing £12.49?

b   Tom has £9.75 and buys 2 books. One book costs £5.29 and the other costs £2.45.
How much money does he have left?

4 Think.

Use £1, 10p and 1p coins.

Take 11 coins. Make up a value, e.g.: five £1 coins, four 10p coins and two 1p coins to make £5.42.

Make up 4 different values in this way.

a   Use the values to make 5 different addition and subtraction calculations.

b   Find the largest and smallest total you can make using any 2 values from 11 coins.

c   Now investigate the largest and smallest difference.

Teacher's Guide

See page 141 of the *Teacher's Guide* for ideas of how to guide practice. Work through each step together as a class to develop children's conceptual understanding.

127 ★

Applying methods of addition and subtraction

You need:
- place-value counters
- Base 10 apparatus

Let's learn

These numbers are all really large. I will need to use a written method.

3250
4255
2100
6000

No, the numbers are multiples of 10, 100 or 1000 so you can use a mental method.

Solving 2-step problems mentally

This word problem is a 2-step problem.

Number of visitors at a theme park.					
	Monday	Tuesday	Wednesday	Thursday	Friday
Visitors	7500	3400	4000	9225	4010

How many more visitors came to the park on Thursday than the total number who came on Tuesday and Wednesday?

The 2 steps are addition and subtraction.

You can represent the problem using a bar model.

Thursday		
Tuesday	Wednesday	?

9225		
3400	4000	?

Step 1: Add 3400 + 4000 to find the total number for Tuesday and Wednesday.

You can use a mental method by simply counting on 4 thousands.

3400 + 4000 = 7400

Step 2: Subtract 7400 from 9225 to find the difference. Use a number line to count on.

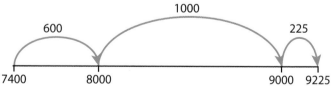

The difference is 600 + 1000 + 225 = 1825.

The answer to the problem is 1825 more visitors.

Teacher's Guide

Before working through the *Textbook*, study page 142 of the *Teacher's Guide* to see how the concepts should be introduced. Read and discuss the page with the children. Provide concrete resources to support exploration.

Explain to your partner why a mental method is possible.

1

Calculate.

Complete these calculations using a mental method.

Represent each one with place-value counters or Base 10 apparatus.

a $1234 + 2000 =$ c $4055 - 600 =$ e $6999 - 90 =$ g $3000 + 700 =$

b $3456 - 3000 =$ d $4055 + 7 =$ f $4000 + 3456 =$

2

Calculate.

a $1234 + 2000 - 150$

b $4055 - 600 + 1245$

c $6999 - 90 - 900$

d   £3000 add £700 and then subtract £1500.

e   There is 4000 ml of water in a large container. Ana pours in another 3450 ml of water and Tom pours in 550ml. How much water is in the container in total?

3

Solve.

This table shows the number of visitors to a theme park over 2 weeks.

How many more visitors came to the theme park in total on a Monday than on a Tuesday?

	Monday	Tuesday	Wednesday	Thursday	Friday	Saturday	Sunday
Week 1	7500	3198	4000	9225	4010	4400	5674
Week 2	2000	5319	5382	600	5200	4400	
Total	9500		9382		9210		7829

Explain how many steps you will take to solve this problem. Is there more than 1 way to solve it?

Make up a 2-step problem of your own using the table.

Ask your partner to solve it.

4

Think.

This bar model shows a 2-step calculation.

The answer is 250.

How many different ways can you make this true?

Try to make calculations that would use a mental strategy.

4-digit number		
?	?	250

Teacher's Guide   See page 143 of the *Teacher's Guide* for ideas of how to guide practice. Work through each step together as a class to develop children's conceptual understanding.

129 ★

Money boards

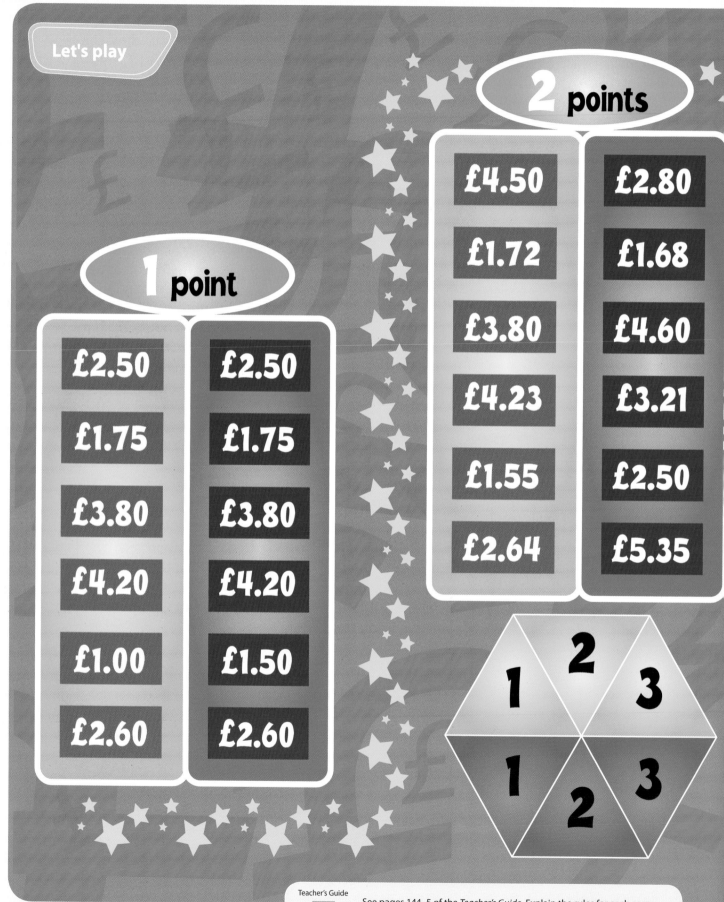

2 points

£4.50	£2.80
£1.72	£1.68
£3.80	£4.60
£4.23	£3.21
£1.55	£2.50
£2.64	£5.35

1 point

£2.50	£2.50
£1.75	£1.75
£3.80	£3.80
£4.20	£4.20
£1.00	£1.50
£2.60	£2.60

Teacher's Guide

See pages 144–5 of the *Teacher's Guide*. Explain the rules for each game and allow children to choose which to play. Encourage them to challenge themselves and practise what they have learnt in the unit.

3 points

£2.48	£5.56
£1.79	£1.75
£3.86	£3.87
£4.28	£4.22
£5.53	£3.94
£2.67	£2.65

You need:

- 1–6 dice
- paperclip and pencil
- calculator

1 **Target 12**
Add amounts from the boards. Who will be the first to get 12 points?

2 **Making a difference**
Subtract amounts from the boards to find the difference.

3 **Your game**
Make up your own game using the gameboard. Explain the rules and play with a partner.

And finally ...

Let's review

⭐ 1

I think all my calculations are correct!

Do you agree with Ana? Explain your answer.

You need:
- place-value grid
- Base 10 apparatus

a
```
  £
  3 . 4 5
+ 1 . 6 2
  4 . 0 7
```

b
```
  £
  1 3 .³4 ¹5
− 1 1 . 2 7
    2 . 1 2
```

c
```
  £
  4 . 3 8
+     1 . 6
  4 . 5 4
```

For any calculations that are not correct, explain Ana's error.

⭐ 2

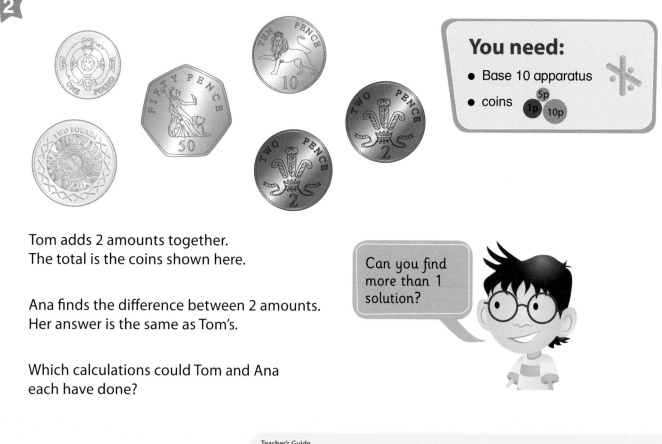

Tom adds 2 amounts together.
The total is the coins shown here.

Ana finds the difference between 2 amounts.
Her answer is the same as Tom's.

Which calculations could Tom and Ana
each have done?

You need:
- Base 10 apparatus
- coins 5p 1p 10p

Can you find more than 1 solution?

Teacher's Guide

See pages 146–7 of the *Teacher's Guide* for guidance on running each task.
Observe children to identify those who have mastered concepts and those who
require further consolidation.

3

£12.75

£9.49

£5.25

You need:
- Base 10 apparatus
- place-value counters
- coins

Tom buys the scarf and the gloves.
Ann buys the hat.

How much more has Tom spent than Anna?

Estimate the answer before you do each calculation.

How can you check your answer?

Did you know?

Did you know that the 1 pence coin was not always the smallest value of coin we used?

Yes! My gran remembers spending halfpenny coins.

Decimals and fractions in real life

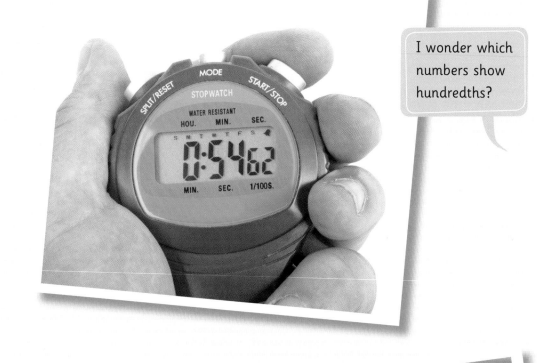

I wonder which numbers show hundredths?

What fraction of a metre is 1 centimetre?

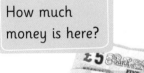

If I wanted half the watermelon and half the pie would I get the same number of pieces?

How much money is here?

If each glass holds 750 ml, I wonder what the total volume is?

Teacher's Guide
Look at the pictures with the children and discuss the questions.
See pages 148–9 of the *Teacher's Guide* for key ideas to draw out.

135

Equivalences

You need:
- interlocking cubes
- ruler
- tape measure

I think 0.25 is the same as $\frac{25}{100}$. We can reduce that to $\frac{2.5}{10}$.

0.25 is the same as $\frac{25}{100}$ but we can't reduce it to $\frac{2.5}{10}$. The numerator of a fraction can't be another fraction. 0.25 is also $\frac{1}{4}$.

Equivalent fractions

Look at the fraction models. They show that $\frac{1}{5}$, $\frac{2}{10}$ and $\frac{3}{15}$ are equivalent.

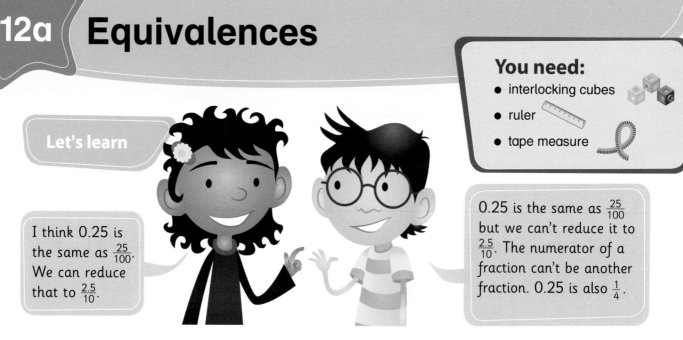

It is easy to add and subtract fractions with the same denominator.

The denominator stays the same. Just add or subtract the numerator.

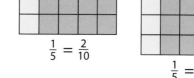

$$\frac{1}{5}$$

$$\frac{1}{5} = \frac{2}{10}$$

$$\frac{1}{5} = \frac{3}{15}$$

Use diagrams or paper strips to show why these fraction statements are true.

$$\frac{7}{15} + \frac{8}{15} = \frac{15}{15} = 1 \qquad\qquad 2\frac{2}{15} - 1\frac{4}{15} = 1\frac{17}{15} - 1\frac{4}{15} = \frac{13}{15}$$

Equivalent fractions and decimals

1									
$\frac{1}{10}$	$\frac{1}{10}$	$\frac{1}{10}$	$\frac{1}{10}$	$\frac{1}{10}$	$\frac{1}{10}$	$\frac{1}{10}$	$\frac{1}{10}$	$\frac{1}{10}$	$\frac{1}{10}$
0.1	0.1	0.1	0.1	0.1	0.1	0.1	0.1	0.1	0.1

A tenth is 1 divided by 10.
$\frac{1}{10}$ is equivalent to 0.1.
Count 7 tenths on the wall. $\frac{7}{10}$ is equivalent to 0.7.

A hundredth is a tenth divided by 10.
So $\frac{7}{100}$ is equivalent to 0.07.

Teacher's Guide

Before working through the *Textbook*, study page 150 of the *Teacher's Guide* to see how the concepts should be introduced. Read and discuss the page with the children. Provide concrete resources to support exploration.

Explain how you found these.

1

Write.

Write down 4 equivalent fractions for each of these:

a $\frac{1}{5}$ c $\frac{1}{10}$ e $\frac{5}{10}$ g $\frac{9}{15}$

b $\frac{2}{5}$ d $\frac{3}{10}$ f $\frac{5}{15}$ h $\frac{12}{15}$

Write these fractions as equivalent decimal fractions:

i $\frac{1}{10}$ j $\frac{7}{10}$ k $\frac{1}{2}$ l $\frac{3}{4}$ m $\frac{15}{100}$

2

Change any improper fractions to mixed numbers.

Calculate.

Make 1 addition statement and 1 subtraction statement for each pair of fractions. Solve your statements.

a $\frac{4}{5}$ and $\frac{3}{5}$ d $1\frac{1}{5}$ and $2\frac{3}{5}$ g $3\frac{1}{10}$ and $2\frac{4}{10}$

b $\frac{9}{15}$ and $\frac{7}{15}$ e $3\frac{2}{5}$ and $1\frac{4}{5}$ h $4\frac{6}{15}$ and $3\frac{13}{15}$

c $\frac{7}{10}$ and $\frac{9}{10}$ f $2\frac{3}{10}$ and $1\frac{7}{10}$

3

Measure.

Find some items in your classroom that you think are over 1 metre in length.

Draw a table. Write down each item. Then add:

a   Your estimate of its length.

b   Its actual length. Measure and record using decimal notation.

c   The difference between your estimate and the actual measurement.

4

Think.

Use these domino patterns as fractions.

a   Draw those that are equivalent.

b   Pick a row and order them from least to greatest.

c   Add those with the same denominator. Write your answers as mixed numbers.

Teacher's Guide

See page 151 of the *Teacher's Guide* for ideas of how to guide practice. Work through each step together as a class to develop children's conceptual understanding.

137

12b Comparing and rounding decimals

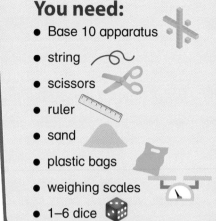

Let's learn

12.5 is larger than 12.4 because 5 is bigger than 4.

But they are not whole numbers. 0.5 is $\frac{5}{10}$ and 0.4 is $\frac{4}{10}$. So 12.5 is larger than 12.4 because 0.5 is bigger than 0.4. We need to use the right vocabulary.

Comparing numbers with decimal places

It is as easy to compare numbers with decimal places as it is to compare whole numbers. Look at the chart. As you move along each row, the numbers get bigger.

10	20	30	40	50	60	70	80	90
1	2	3	4	5	6	7	8	9
0.1	0.2	0.3	0.4	0.5	0.6	0.7	0.8	0.9
0.01	0.02	0.03	0.04	0.05	0.06	0.07	0.08	0.09

Look at the pictures of the Base 10 apparatus. They show 2.6 and 2.8.

They have the same number of ones, but 2.8 has more tenths.

So 2.8 > 2.6 or 2.6 < 2.8.

2.6   2.8

Rounding decimals

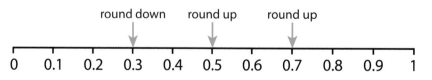

round down   round up   round up

0   0.1   0.2   0.3   0.4   0.5   0.6   0.7   0.8   0.9   1

Rounding decimals is the same as rounding whole numbers.

26.3 is rounded down to 26 because the tenth digit is lower than 5.

31.5 is rounded up to 32 because the tenth digit is 5.

12.6 is rounded up to 13 because the tenth digit is higher than 5.

1 Compare.

Write 2 statements for each pair of numbers. Use the < and > symbols.

Try these!

a   1.3 and 1.7   e   94.8 and 94.1

b   1.8 and 1.4   f   41.19 and 41.13

c   5.9 and 5.8   g   53.84 and 53.85   i   64.3 and 64.18

d   17.5 and 17.7   h   75.26 and 75.36   j   87.68 and 87.6

Now find 2 ways to make them equal, e.g. 2.4 = 0.4 = 2.8 and 2.8 -0.4 - 2.4

2 Round.

Try these!

Round each of these numbers to the nearest whole number.

a   1.4   c   7.9   e   15.5   g   35.8   i   2.31

b   3.6   d   12.1   f   26.2   h   42.5   j   4.67

3 Measure.

a   Cut 6 lengths of string. Measure them to the nearest millimetre. Record the lengths. Round to the nearest centimetre and record beside the actual lengths.

b   Put some sand in 5 plastic bags. Weigh them. Record their masses. Round the masses to the nearest tenth and then kilogram. Record these beside the actual masses.

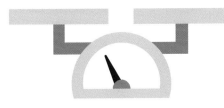

4 Think.

Tom throws 2 dice. If the numbers are the same, he throws again. If the numbers are different, he uses them to make 2 decimal numbers.

Here are the first numbers he makes:

1.5 and 5.1

3.6 and 6.3

4.2 and 2.4

He rounds the numbers to the nearest whole number. He thinks that, whatever numbers he makes, he will never be able to round them to the same whole number. Is Tom correct? Explain your thinking.

Teacher's Guide   See page 153 of the *Teacher's Guide* for ideas of how to guide practice. Work through each step together as a class to develop children's conceptual understanding.

139

Fraction frenzy

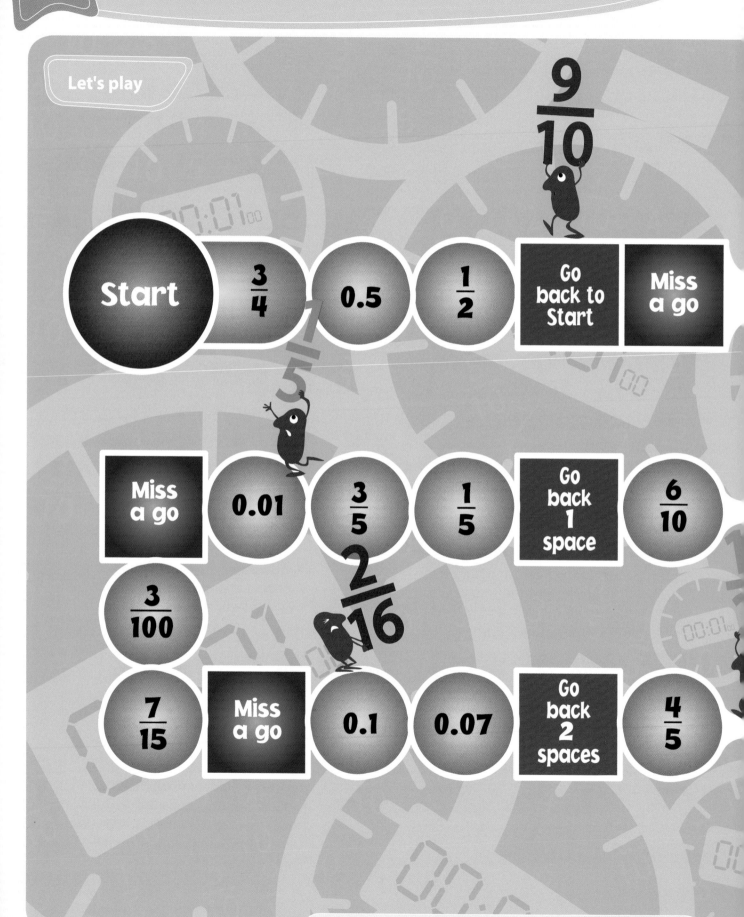

Let's play

Start

$\frac{3}{4}$

0.5

$\frac{1}{2}$

Go back to Start

Miss a go

$\frac{9}{10}$

Miss a go

0.01

$\frac{3}{5}$

$\frac{1}{5}$

Go back 1 space

$\frac{6}{10}$

$\frac{3}{100}$

$\frac{2}{16}$

$\frac{7}{15}$

Miss a go

0.1

0.07

Go back 2 spaces

$\frac{4}{5}$

Teacher's Guide

See pages 154–5 of the *Teacher's Guide*. Explain the rules for each game and allow children to choose which to play. Encourage them to challenge themselves and practise what they have learnt in the unit.

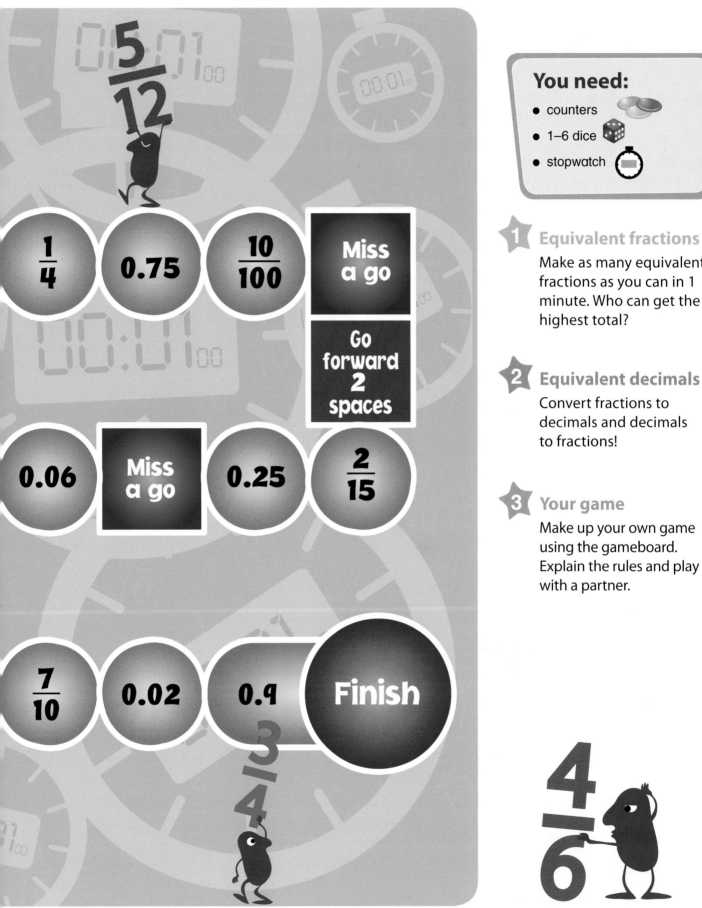

141

And finally ...

Let's review

1

Write down 5 equivalent fractions for each of these.

a $\frac{1}{5}$ c $\frac{1}{15}$ e $\frac{3}{15}$ g $\frac{8}{10}$

b $\frac{1}{10}$ d $\frac{4}{5}$ f $\frac{12}{15}$ h $\frac{5}{10}$

Make 1 addition statement and 1 subtraction statement for each pair of fractions.

i $\frac{1}{5}$ and $\frac{2}{5}$ m $1\frac{3}{10}$ and $1\frac{1}{10}$

j $\frac{7}{10}$ and $\frac{1}{10}$ n $3\frac{7}{10}$ and $1\frac{9}{10}$

k $\frac{3}{15}$ and $\frac{7}{15}$ o $4\frac{1}{5}$ and $2\frac{4}{5}$

l $\frac{13}{15}$ and $\frac{5}{15}$ p $5\frac{3}{15}$ and $3\frac{7}{15}$

Solve your statements.

2

Convert these fractions to decimals.

a $\frac{1}{4}$ d $\frac{9}{10}$ g $\frac{3}{100}$ j $\frac{48}{100}$

b $\frac{3}{4}$ e $\frac{7}{10}$ h $\frac{15}{100}$ k $\frac{95}{100}$

c $\frac{1}{2}$ f $\frac{1}{100}$ i $\frac{25}{100}$ l $\frac{55}{100}$

Change these decimals to fractions.

m 0.3   p 0.4   s 0.12   v 0.72

n 0.5   q 0.07   t 0.25   w 0.36

o 0.1   r 0.08   u 0.65   x 0.24

Teacher's Guide

See pages 156–7 of the *Teacher's Guide* for guidance on running each task.
Observe children to identify those who have mastered concepts and those who require further consolidation.

3

Write 2 statements for each pair of numbers.
Use the < and > symbols.

a   2.4 and 2.8

b   6.9 and 6.3

c   12.25 and 12.35

d   24.68 and 24.28

e   25.34 and 25.35

f   36.12 and 36.17

Round each of these numbers to the nearest whole number.

g   6.7

h   8.3

i   12.6

j   15.1

k   24.5

l   32.9

Draw a number line to help you.

Did you know?

A lot of the mathematical vocabulary we use comes from an old language called Latin.

The word 'fraction' comes from the Latin word *fractio* which means 'to break'.
'Decimal' comes from the Latin *decimus* meaning 'tenth'.

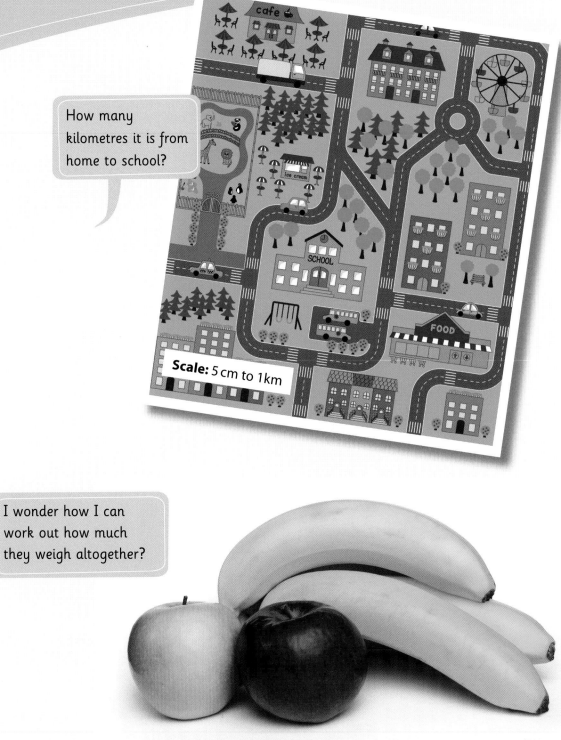

How many kilometres it is from home to school?

Scale: 5 cm to 1 km

I wonder how I can work out how much they weigh altogether?

Mass of fruit

Bananas	100 g each
Apples	70 g each

How many times bigger does the photo need to be to fit this frame?

How many different outfits could someone choose to wear?

I scored 45 points on the first level of my computer game. I wonder what my total will be if I score that on the first 8 levels?

Teacher's Guide

Look at the pictures with the children and discuss the questions.
See pages 158–9 of the *Teacher's Guide* for key ideas to draw out.

13a | Multiplying and dividing mentally

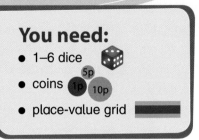

You need:
- 1–6 dice
- coins 5p 1p 10p
- place-value grid

Let's learn

I can count in 25s from 4:
4, 25, 50, 75 ...

You made a mistake! You need to count in 25s from your starting number. You should have counted 4, 29, 54, 79 ...

Count in 25s and 1000s

The blue jumps are steps of 25.

Each step only lands on numbers ending 00, 25, 50 or 75.

The red jumps are steps of 100.

1 red jump is equivalent to 4 blue jumps. $4 \times 25 = 100$

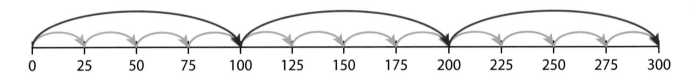

You can count in multiples of 1000 from any number.

These numbers go up in steps of 2000 from 1045. The digits in the thousands column increase by 2 each time.

1000	100	10	1
1	0	4	5
3	0	4	5
5	0	4	5
7	0	4	5
9	0	4	5

Recall all multiplication tables

There are connections between multiplication tables.

Use what you know to work out other multiplication facts.

I know that $2 \times 3 = 6$. So, I also know that:
$2 \times 6 = 12 \rightarrow 2 \times 12 = 24 \rightarrow 4 \times 12 = 48 \rightarrow 8 \times 12 = 96$

Teacher's Guide

Before working through the *Textbook*, study page 160 of the *Teacher's Guide* to see how the concepts should be introduced. Read and discuss the page with the children. Provide concrete resources to support exploration.

1

Calculate.

a $6 \times 25 =$

b   What is 5000 more than 21 701?

c $19 \times 25 =$

d   What is 2000 less than 41 602?

e $625 = 25 \times$ ☐

f $825 \div$ ☐ $= 75$

g $125, 150,$ ☐ $,$ ☐ $, 225$

2

Answer these.

Copy and complete:

a $2 \times 4 = 8$. So, $2 \times 8 =$ ☐

b $3 \times 5 =$ ☐ . So, $6 \times 5 =$ ☐

c $3 \times 7 = 21$. So, $6 \times 7 =$ ☐

d $4 \times 3 =$ ☐ . So, $4 \times$ ☐ $= 24$
    and $4 \times$ ☐ $= 48$

e $6 \div 2 = 3$. So, $12 \div 2 =$ ☐

f $30 \div 3 = 10$. So, $60 \div$ ☐ $= 20$

3

Solve.

This pictogram shows how many points 5 children scored in a game of snap.

Ana	▩ ▩ ▩
Tom	▩ ▩ ▮
Fay	▩ ▩
Jon	▩ ▩ ▪
Sam	▩ ▩ ▮

▩ represents 6

a   How many points did Jon score?

b   Which 2 children scored the same number of points?

c   How many more points has Ana scored than Fay?

d   How many points have been scored altogether?

e   Jim scores 28 points. Draw the pictogram for his score.

4

Think.

a   Roll a dice 3 times to get a 3-digit number. Try to reach this target number using:
  • 3, 6, 8, 25 and 100 up to once each
  • any of the 4 operations.

b   Find as many ways as you can to work out the multiplication facts for 7 using your knowledge of the other multiplication tables.

Teacher's Guide
See page 161 of the *Teacher's Guide* for ideas of how to guide practice. Work through each step together as a class to develop children's conceptual understanding.

147

Multiplying on paper

You need:
- number rods
- place-value counters

Let's learn

Look at how I worked out 347 × 6. The answer's 1882.

$$\begin{array}{r} 347 \\ \times \quad 6 \\ \hline 1882 \\ {\scriptstyle 2\ 4} \end{array}$$

No it isn't. You forgot to add the 200 on to 1800. It should be 2082.

Column method for 3-digit numbers

You can use the grid method to multiply a 3-digit number.

Work out the hundreds, tens and ones, then add the results.

You can also use the column method.

Start with the ones.

Work out $7 \times 4 = 28$.

Carry the 2 tens into the tens column.

Work out $80 \times 4 = 320$.

Add the carried tens to give 340.

Carry the 3 hundreds into the hundreds column.

Finally, work out $500 \times 4 = 2000$.

Add the carried hundreds to give 2300. The answer is 2348.

587

×	500	80	7
4	2000	320	28

$587 \times 4 = 2000 + 320 + 28 = 2348$

$$\begin{array}{r} 587 \\ \times \quad 4 \\ \hline 2348 \\ {\scriptstyle 3\ 2} \end{array} \qquad \begin{array}{r} 587 \\ \times \quad 4 \\ \hline 2348 \\ {\scriptstyle 3\ 2} \end{array} \qquad \begin{array}{r} 587 \\ \times \quad 4 \\ \hline 2348 \\ {\scriptstyle 3\ 2} \end{array} \qquad \begin{array}{r} 587 \\ \times \quad 4 \\ \hline 2348 \\ {\scriptstyle 3\ 2} \end{array}$$

Solving problems

The bar model can help make sense of problems involving multiplication and its inverse.

Tom bought 3 gobstoppers and 2 toffees.

The gobstoppers cost 6p each. He spend 32p in total.

How much did 1 toffee cost?

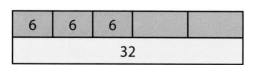

To find the length of the 2 pink bars:

work out $6 \times 3 = 18$ and then subtract 18 from 32.

$32 - 18 = 14$ so the 2 pink bars equal 14.

$14 \div 2 = 7$ so 1 pink bar equals 7.

1 toffee cost 7p.

Teacher's Guide

Before working through the *Textbook*, study page 162 of the *Teacher's Guide* to see how the concepts should be introduced. Read and discuss the page with the children. Provide concrete resources to support exploration.

1

Calculate.

Copy and complete.

a $243 \times 5 =$

b $608 \times 7 =$

c $831 \times 6 =$

d
$$
\begin{array}{r}
3\,2\,1 \\
\times \quad \underline{} \\
1\,9\,2\,6 \\
\hline
1
\end{array}
$$

e
$$
\begin{array}{r}
5\,8 \\
\times \quad \underline{4} \\
2\,3\,2\,8 \\
\hline
3
\end{array}
$$

f
$$
\begin{array}{r}
3\,4 \\
\times \quad \underline{} \\
4\,4\,3\,8 \\
\hline
2\,\,2
\end{array}
$$

2

Calculate.

Copy and complete.

a $25 \times 5 + 75 \times 2 =$

b $4 \times 7 + 6 \times 12 =$

c $7 \times 8 = 7 \times 3 + 7 \times \boxed{}$

d $7 \times 6 = 10 \times 6 - 3 \times \boxed{}$

e $58 = 23 + 5 \times \boxed{}$

Remember, always multiply before you add or subtract. Draw bar models to help you.

3

Solve.

Use your knowledge of multiplying and adding to solve these problems.

a   Tom has 6 pieces of string. Each one is 429 cm long. What is the total length of string he has?

b   Ana walks 358 m to school and the same distance back each day. How far does she walk to get to and from school in 4 days?

c   Tom runs 7 laps of the running track. Each lap is 428 m. How far does he run altogether?

d   6 eggs weighing 48 g each are placed in a bowl. The mass of the bowl and its contents is 503 g. How much does the bowl weigh?

e   Ana buys 4 apples weighing 120 g each and 3 oranges. The total mass of the fruit is 885 g. What is the mass of each orange?

4

Think.

$\boxed{} \times 3 + 7 \times \boxed{} = 41$

What pairs of numbers can go in the boxes to make this true?

Write some word problems that can be modelled with this bar model.

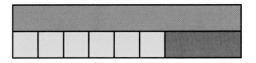

Teacher's Guide

See page 163 of the *Teacher's Guide* for ideas of how to guide practice. Work through each step together as a class to develop children's conceptual understanding.

149 ⭐

Let's learn

I have 3 scarves and 2 hats. There are 5 combinations that I can wear.

That's not right! There are 6 combinations. For each hat there are 3 scarves to choose from, so $2 \times 3 = 6$ combinations.

Scaling with whole numbers

The purple bar is 5 times as long as the green bar.

If the green bar is worth 4, then the purple bar is worth $5 \times 4 = 20$.

If the green bar is worth 60, then the purple bar is worth $5 \times 60 = 300$.

If the purple bar is worth 60, then the green bar is worth 12 because $5 \times 12 = 60$.

Correspondence problems

Correspondence problems are about comparing different sized sets so that one set has m objects and the other has n objects and m and n are either multiplied or divided.

Ana is making goody bags for a party.

Each goody bag contains a hat, a balloon and a whistle.

She has 2 colours of each.

She uses this diagram to make a list of all the different combinations she can make.

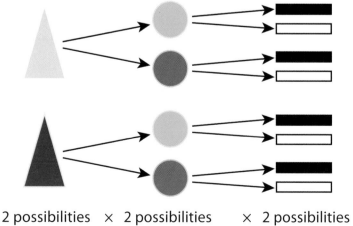

Hat	Balloon	Whistle
Blue	Green	Black
Blue	Green	White
Blue	Purple	Black
Blue	Purple	White
Red	Green	Black
Red	Green	White
Red	Purple	Black
Red	Purple	White

2 possibilities × 2 possibilities × 2 possibilities = 8 possibilities

Teacher's Guide

Before working through the *Textbook*, study page 164 of the *Teacher's Guide* to see how the concepts should be introduced. Read and discuss the page with the children. Provide concrete resources to support exploration.

1

Answer these.

Calculate.

Copy and complete.

a   What is 3 times as large as 6?

d   42 is ____ times as large as 6.

b   What is 7 times as much as 9?

e   72 is 9 times as large as ____ .

c   What is 12 times as much as 4?

f   ____ is 8 times as large as 12.

2

Answer these.

a   A menu has 2 starters, 3 main courses and 4 puddings. How many different 3 course meals could you choose from?

b   A pattern consists of 3 tiles in a row. Each tile could be one of 3 colours. How many different patterns could be made?

3

Solve.

You want to make a scale model of your classroom.

Measure the length, width and height of the classroom. Measure to the nearest metre.

Your measurements must be 10 times smaller in the model. Work out the dimensions of the model.

4

Tom is making ice-cream cones for his classmates. He wants to make a different ice-cream cone for each of the 15 children.

He has waffle cones and chocolate cones. Each cone will have 1 scoop of ice-cream. How many flavours does he need?

Investigate how many flavours of ice-cream he needs if:

a   There are 24 children

b   Each ice-cream cone has 2 scoops of ice cream.

Make sure you measure the windows and doors, too! Does your model make sense?

Teacher's Guide
See page 165 of the *Teacher's Guide* for ideas of how to guide practice. Work through each step together as a class to develop children's conceptual understanding.

151 ⭐

Terrific tables

Start 1 2 3 4

Finish 15 14 13 12

Teacher's Guide

See pages 166–7 of the *Teacher's Guide*. Explain the rules for each game and allow children to choose which to play. Encourage them to challenge themselves and practise what they have learnt in the unit.

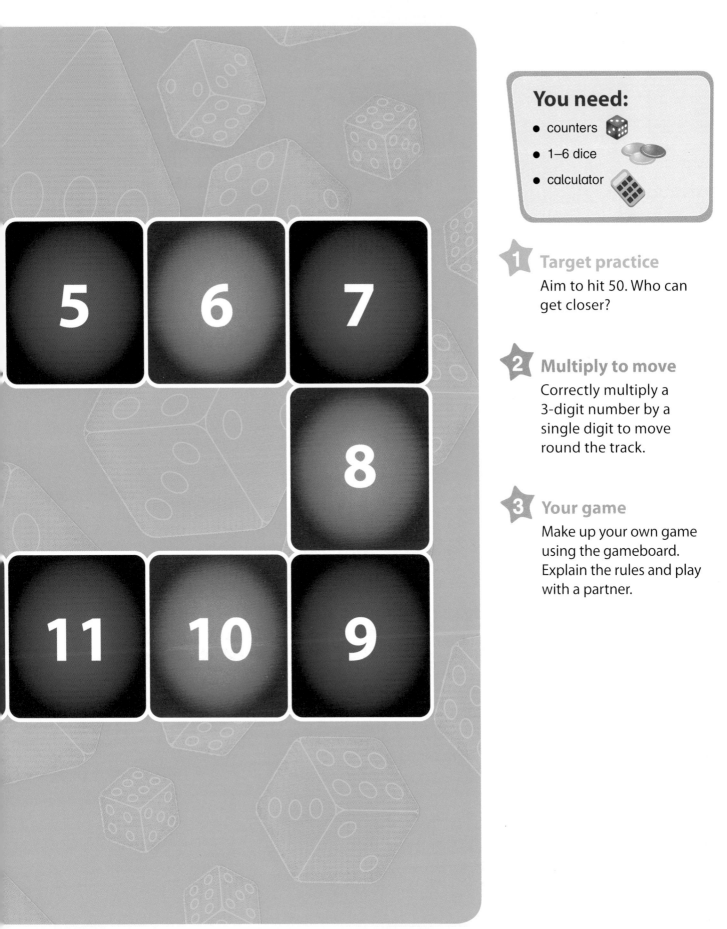

You need:

- counters
- 1–6 dice
- calculator

1 Target practice

Aim to hit 50. Who can get closer?

2 Multiply to move

Correctly multiply a 3-digit number by a single digit to move round the track.

3 Your game

Make up your own game using the gameboard. Explain the rules and play with a partner.

And finally ...

1

Ana has got all her homework questions wrong.

Work out the correct answers.
Then write some feedback to explain to Ana where she went wrong.

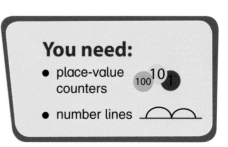

You need:
- place-value counters 100 10 1
- number lines

a   Count up in steps of 25, starting at 3 and ending on the step after 200.

3, 25, 50, 75, 100, 125, 150, 175, 200, 225

b   What is three thousand more than 4601?

4901

c   Work out 418×7 using short multiplication.

$$
\begin{array}{r}
418 \\
\times7 \\
\hline
28126 \\
5
\end{array}
$$

d   Apples cost 45p each and pears cost 60p each. How much do 4 apples and 5 pears cost?

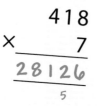

$45 + 60 = 105$

$105 \times 9 = 945p = £9.45$

e   Tom has 5 counters and Ana has 4 times as many. How many do they have altogether?

They have 9 counters altogether.

Teacher's Guide   See pages 168–9 of the *Teacher's Guide* for guidance on running each task. Observe children to identify those who have mastered concepts and those who require further consolidation.

★**154**

2

A code to open a door in a computer game has 4 positions.
Each one can be either red or blue.

How many different codes are there?
Can you list them all?

What if there are 5 positions?
Can you find a quick way to work out the number of possible codes?
Can you explain why it works?

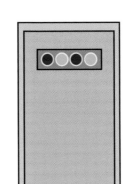

You need:
● counters

3

Write down a 2-digit number.
Reverse the digits to make another 2-digit number.
Add the two 2-digit numbers together.

Repeat with another 2-digit number.
What do you notice? Why do you think that is?

Now instead of adding them,
find the difference between them.

You need:
● calculator
● place-value counters

What do you notice? Why do you think it happens?

Did you know?

The first people to use multiplication tables were the Babylonians, about 4000 years ago.

They wrote them on tablets and carried them around with them. They used the tablets to do calculations when they were trading goods.

Perimeter, area and symmetry

I wonder how farmers calculate how much fencing they need?

How can you describe this car park?

Why are line markings so important in team games?

I wonder if lines of symmetry can be in any direction?

How do the people in the photo know where to stand?

Teacher's Guide

Look at the pictures with the children and discuss the questions.
See pages 170–1 of the *Teacher's Guide* for key ideas to draw out.

157 ★

Perimeter and area

Let's learn

You need:
- squared paper
- ruler
- metre stick or tape measure

The perimeter of a 3 cm square is 12 cm. Its area is 9 cm.

Yes, the perimeter is 12 cm but the area is 9 cm² (centimetres squared). Area is measured in square units because it measures surface.

Area

Area is the size of a surface. It is measured in 'square' units (mm², cm², m², km²).

The area of the green square is 1 square centimetre.
You write this 1 cm² and read it as '1 centimetre squared'.

1 cm / 1 cm

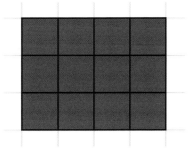

12 green squares would cover this rectangle.
Area of rectangle = 12 cm²

9 green squares would cover this square.
Area of square = 9 cm²

Perimeter of a rectangle using algebra

Perimeter is the total distance around the outside of a shape.
It is measured in centimetres or metres.

Here are 3 ways of writing the perimeter using algebra.

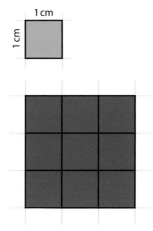

4 cm / a

2 cm b   b 2 cm

a
4 cm

Perimeter = 4 cm + 2 cm + 4 cm + 2 cm = 12 cm $P = a + b + a + b$

Perimeter = 2 × 4 cm + 2 × 2 cm = 12 cm $P = 2a + 2b$

Perimeter = 2 × (4 cm + 2 cm) = 12 cm $P = 2(a + b)$

Teacher's Guide

Before working through the *Textbook*, study page 172 of the *Teacher's Guide* to see how the concepts should be introduced. Read and discuss the page with the children. Provide concrete resources to support exploration.

1

Calculate.

Find the perimeter and area of these shapes. Each square is 1 cm.

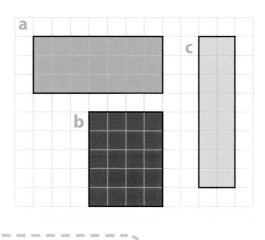

d   Square with sides of 5 cm.

e   Rectangle with length 9 cm and width 1 cm.

2

Draw.

Draw diagrams on squared paper to show the missing measurements.

a   A square has an area of 16 cm². Show the length of its sides.

b   The length of a patio is 6 m. The area is 12 m². Show the width of the patio.

c   2 different rectangles have a perimeter of 10 cm. Show their lengths and widths. Find their areas.

d   2 different rectangles that have an area of 6 cm². Show their lengths and widths. Find their perimeters.

3

Measure.

Look at the display boards in your classroom.

Measure the length and width in centimetres. Round to the nearest 10 cm. Calculate the cost of covering the boards in your classroom.

Silver edging £1.00 per m²

Coloured backing fabric £5.00 per m²

4

Think.

Copy and complete the table. Show the perimeter and area of squares as they increase in size.

Length of side	1 cm	2 cm	3 cm	4 cm	5 cm	6 cm	7 cm	8 cm	9 cm	10 cm
Perimeter										
Area										

Describe any patterns you can see in the answers.

Teacher's Guide

See page 173 of the *Teacher's Guide* for ideas of how to guide practice. Work through each step together as a class to develop children's conceptual understanding.

159 ★

Perimeter and angles

Let's learn

When I'm finding the perimeter of a shape, I'm never sure if I've added up all the sides.

I mark one corner and trace round the shape with my finger. That helps.

Perimeter of rectilinear shapes

A rectilinear shape is a composite shape made of simple rectangles.

All the angles in a rectilinear shape are right angles.

To find the perimeter, start in one corner, for example, the top left-hand corner (S). Move clockwise around the shape.

Total the length of each of the sides.

In these diagrams, each square represents 1 cm².

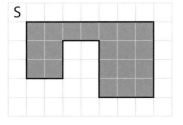

$P = 7\,cm + 4\,cm + 3\,cm + 3\,cm + 2\,cm + 2\,cm + 2\,cm + 3\,cm = 26\,cm$

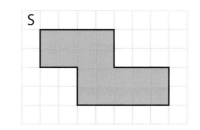

$P = 4\,cm + 2\,cm + 3\,cm + 2\,cm + 5\,cm + 2\,cm + 2\,cm + 2\,cm = 22\,cm$

Comparing angles

Angles are an amount of turn. They are measured in degrees.

To help you order acute and obtuse angles you can visualise a right angle, half a right angle and one and a half right angles.

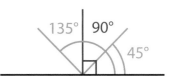

Two right angles make a straight line angle.

1 Calculate.

Calculate the perimeters of each shape.

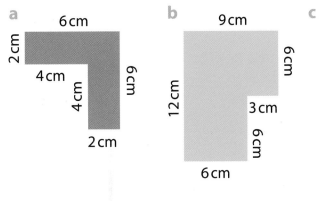

a

6 cm
2 cm
4 cm
4 cm
6 cm
2 cm

b

9 cm
6 cm
12 cm
3 cm
6 cm
6 cm

c

Draw your own symmetrical cross shape similar to the one below. Calculate the perimeter.

2 Order.

Describe the angles in each polygon. Write them in order, starting with the smallest.

a

b
a c

b

d
e
e
f
f

c

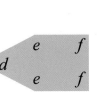

i
h
g j

3 Apply.

You have 24 square patio slabs. Each measures 1 m².

How many different ways can you arrange them?

Calculate the perimeter of each way.

Which has the largest perimeter? Which has the smallest?

Can you explain why?

4 Investigate.

Work with a partner.

Roll 6 centimetre cubes on cm² paper. Mark their positions.

Find the rectilinear shape with the smallest perimeter around the positions.

None of the cube positions can touch the perimeter.

Does your shape have the smallest possible area?

Teacher's Guide   See page 175 of the *Teacher's Guide* for ideas of how to guide practice. Work through each step together as a class to develop children's conceptual understanding.

161

14c Area and symmetry

You need:
- mirror
- cm² paper
- ruler
- blue and yellow pencils

Let's learn

Why are you **multiplying** to find the area? You need to **count** the squares.

Counting squares to find the area does always work. If it's a simple rectangle, you can also multiply the number of squares in the length by the number of squares in the width.

Area arrays

You can find the area of shapes by counting squares.

Rectangle A is an array of 2 rows of 3 squares. 3 × 2 = 6, giving an area of 6 cm².

Rectangle B is an array of 3 rows of 4 squares. 4 × 3 = 12, giving an area of 12 cm².

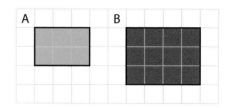

Using multiplication is easier when there are lots of squares to count.
Here 10 rows of 10 make 100 squares so the area is 100 cm².

Completing a symmetrical figure

To complete the other half of the diagram, start at the line of symmetry and colour the same pattern on the other side.

Use the squares in each line to check both sides are exactly the same.

When a symmetrical figure is folded along the line of symmetry the 2 halves fit exactly.

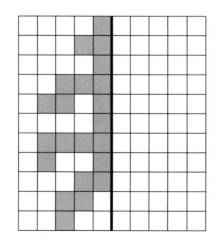

Teacher's Guide

Before working through the *Textbook*, study page 176 of the *Teacher's Guide* to see how the concepts should be introduced. Read and discuss the page with the children. Provide concrete resources to support exploration.

★162

1 Answer these.

Find the area of these shapes. Each square is 1 cm.

Explain your method.

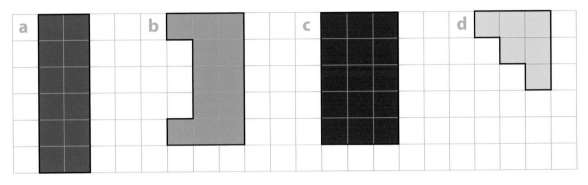

2 Plot.

Draw a coordinate grid with x- and y-axes labelled 0–10.

Draw a mirror line at $x = 5$.

Each shape is half of a symmetrical polygon.

Complete each polygon and name it.

List the missing coordinates.

a   (4, 1), (2, 2), (4, 3)

b   (5, 5), (3, 6), (4, 7), (3, 8), (5, 9)

3 Draw.

Work with a partner.

On squared paper, draw half a house, half a face and half an insect.

Swap papers. Complete the drawings so they are symmetrical.

4 Investigate.

This diagram shows a rectilinear shape with an area of 10 cm².

Find 8 different ways to draw shapes within a 4 cm × 4 cm square that have an area equal to 10 cm².

Colour the shapes with a line of symmetry yellow.

Colour the shapes with no line of symmetry blue.

Teacher's Guide   See page 177 of the *Teacher's Guide* for ideas of how to guide practice.
Work through each step together as a class to develop children's
conceptual understanding.

163 ★

Rectangle reckoning!

Let's play

1 (0, 0), (1, 0), (0, 7), (1, 7)

2 (3, 9), (3, 10), (7, 9), (7, 10)

3 (13, 13), (13, 15), (15, 13), (15, 15)

6 (3, 6), (3, 8), (6, 6), (6, 8)

7 (3, 11), (3, 15), (6, 11), (6, 15)

8 (9, 0), (10, 0), (9, 3), (10, 3)

11 (4, 0), (5, 0), (4, 5), (5, 5)

12 (14, 9), (15, 9), (14, 11), (15, 11)

13 (1, 14), (1, 15), (2, 14), (2, 15)

16 (2, 1), (2, 5), (3, 1), (3, 5)

17 (9, 5), (9, 8), (15, 5), (15, 8)

18 (11, 13), (11, 15), (12, 13), (12, 15)

Teacher's Guide

See pages 178–9 of the *Teacher's Guide*. Explain the rules for each game and allow children to choose which to play. Encourage them to challenge themselves and practise what they have learnt in the unit.

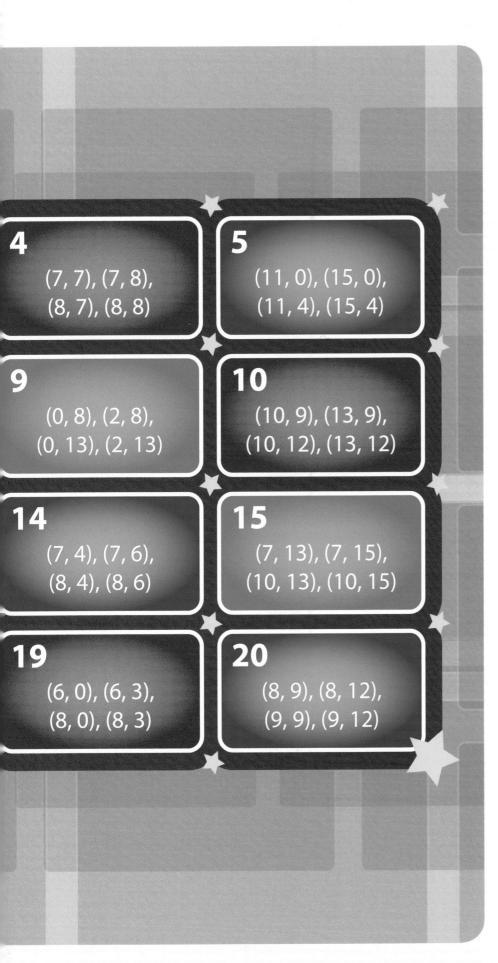

4
(7, 7), (7, 8),
(8, 7), (8, 8)

5
(11, 0), (15, 0),
(11, 4), (15, 4)

9
(0, 8), (2, 8),
(0, 13), (2, 13)

10
(10, 9), (13, 9),
(10, 12), (13, 12)

14
(7, 4), (7, 6),
(8, 4), (8, 6)

15
(7, 13), (7, 15),
(10, 13), (10, 15)

19
(6, 0), (6, 3),
(8, 0), (8, 3)

20
(8, 9), (8, 12),
(9, 9), (9, 12)

You need:
- counters
- 1–20 dice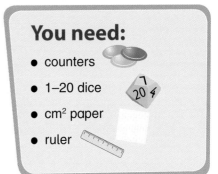
- cm² paper
- ruler

⭐**1** **Perimeter points**
Roll the dice and plot
the rectangle. Find its
perimeter for your score.

⭐**2** **Adding areas**
Roll the dice and plot
the rectangle. Find its
area for your score.

⭐**3** **Your game**
Make up your own game
using the gameboard.
Explain the rules and play
with a partner.

Let's review

1

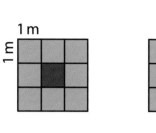

1 m

1 m

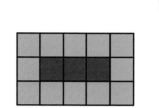

flowerbed

patio

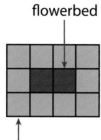

Work with a partner.

Look at the diagrams. Each square has a side of 1 m.

Investigate what happens to the perimeters and areas of the flowerbed and the patio as they increase in size.

You need:
- squared paper
- ruler

Can you find any patterns?

2

Draw a 3 by 3 grid.

Using one colour only, how many symmetrical patterns can you colour:

a with a horizontal line of symmetry like this?

b with a diagonal line of symmetry like this?

You need:
- squared paper
- ruler
- coloured pencil

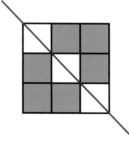

Teacher's Guide

See pages 180–1 of the *Teacher's Guide* for guidance on running each task. Observe children to identify those who have mastered concepts and those who require further consolidation.

3

2 rectangles make an L-shape – an irregular hexagon.

Use some of these rectangles to draw 4 different L-shapes each with a perimeter of 20 cm.

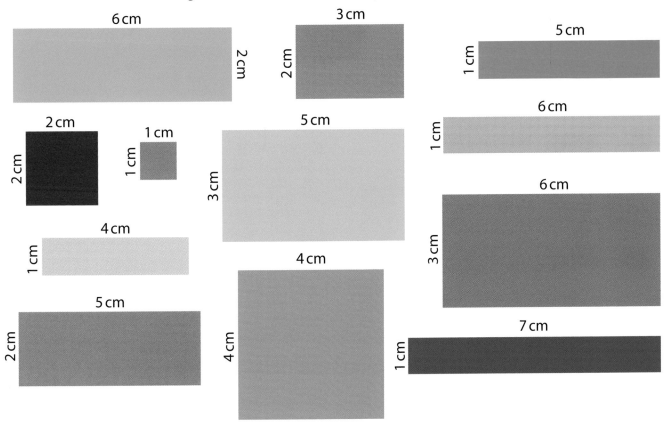

6 cm
2 cm

3 cm
2 cm

5 cm
1 cm

2 cm
2 cm

1 cm
1 cm

5 cm
3 cm

6 cm
1 cm

6 cm
3 cm

4 cm
1 cm

5 cm
2 cm

4 cm
4 cm

7 cm
1 cm

Did you know?

The A4 paper size we use at school has a fixed perimeter and area. It is part of a series of paper sizes from A0 to A10.

A Series Formats Sizes
ISO 216 international standard (ISO) paper sizes

A0 (841×1189)

A1
594 × 841

A2
420 × 594

A3
297 × 420

A4
297 × 210

A5
148 × 210

A6

A7

A0 has an area of 1 m². If you fold A0 in half it gives A1. A2 is half A1, A3 is half A2 and so on.

2-dimensional (2-D)

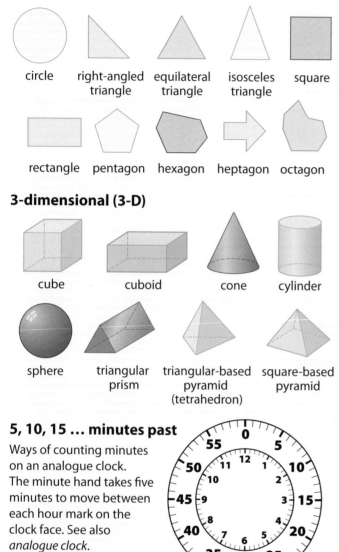

circle | right-angled triangle | equilateral triangle | isosceles triangle | square

rectangle | pentagon | hexagon | heptagon | octagon

3-dimensional (3-D)

cube | cuboid | cone | cylinder

sphere | triangular prism | triangular-based pyramid (tetrahedron) | square-based pyramid

5, 10, 15 … minutes past

Ways of counting minutes on an analogue clock. The minute hand takes five minutes to move between each hour mark on the clock face. See also *analogue clock*.

12-hour time

Counting hours of the day in 2 blocks of twelve. 12.01-12 noon as a.m. and 12.01-12 midnight as p.m. Often told on a 12-hour clock with hands and known as analogue time.

24-hour time

Counting hours of the day from 0-24. Used on digital clocks. 2 p.m. is written as 14:00.

A

above/below zero

Temperatures either above or below freezing point (0°C), e.g. 4° below zero is –4°C. See also *minus*.

acute angle

An angle between 0° and 90°. See also *obtuse, reflex angle*.

addend

The numbers being added together in an addition calculation. Augend + addend = sum (or total).

$$3 + 5 = 8$$
augend   addend   sum/total

analogue clock

A dial with hands used to show time. The dial shows 12 hours in a full circle. The minute hand moves 1 complete turn every circle.

minute hand
hour hand

area

The size of a surface. Measured in 'square' units: mm^2, cm^2, m^2, km^2.

$12cm^2$

array

An arrangement of numbers, shapes or objects in rows of equal size and columns of equal size, used to find out how many altogether.

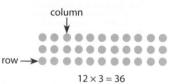

column
row →
$12 \times 3 = 36$

augend

The number being added to in an addition calculation. Augend + addend = sum (or total)

$$3 + 5 = 8$$
augend   addend   sum/total

B

base

The flat surface underneath a 3-D shape, e.g. a square-based pyramid has 1 square base and 4 triangular faces.

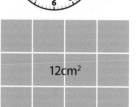

breadth

The same as width.

C

calendar

A list of the days of the year, arranged by month, week and day.

capacity

The amount a container holds. It is measured in litres or millilitres, e.g. the capacity of a 2-litre bottle is 2 litres.

Celsius

A scale used to measure temperature. Sometimes called Centigrade. Units are °C.

centre

A point at the exact middle of a shape.

century

100 years.

commutative

Addition and multiplication are commutative. It does not matter which way you add, mulitply or divide, the answer is always the same. Same answer, different calculation, e.g. 3 + 4 = 4 + 3. But subtraction is not commutative, e.g. 7 − 2 ≠ 2 − 7.

consecutive

Numbers which follow each other in order.

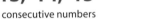

13, 14, 15	**24, 26, 28**
consecutive numbers	consecutive even numbers

cylinder, cylindrical

A 3-D object with circular ends and a uniform cross-section. The top is vertically above the base. Like a cylinder.

D

data

Pieces of information usually represented in a special way, e.g. on bar charts and pie charts.

decimal fraction, decimal equivalent

Fractions as tenths or hundredths are represented as digits after a decimal point, e.g. 0.25 is equivalent to $\frac{1}{4}$ and $\frac{25}{100}$.

degree

A unit used to measure the size of an angle. Symbol: °. There are 360° in one complete turn. Also a unit of temperature.

denominator

The number of parts the whole has been divided into. The number underneath the vinculum. Also called the divisor.

diagonal

A straight line inside a shape that goes from one corner to another (but not an edge).

difference

The result of a subtraction. The difference between 12 and 5 is 7. See also *minuend, subtrahend*.

digital time

Times displayed as on a digital clock, either as 12-hour or 24-hour time.

dividend

The number that is divided in a division sum, e.g. in 12 ÷ 6 = 2, 12 is the dividend. See also *divisor, quotient , division bracket*.

$$\text{dividend} \longrightarrow 12 \div \underset{\uparrow}{6} = 2 \longleftarrow \text{quotient}$$
$$\text{divisor}$$

division bracket

The half box around the dividend in a division. See also *dividend*.

$$16\overline{)2112} \longleftarrow \text{dividend}$$

division bracket

divisor

The number that is used to divide in a division sum, e.g. in 12 ÷ 6 = 2, 6 is the divisor. See also *dividend, quotient*.

E

equilateral triangle

A triangle with 3 equal sides and 3 equal angles of 60°.

equivalent

Two numbers or expressions that are equal, but which can be in a different form, e.g. £1 is equivalent to 100p. Two fractions are equivalent if they have the same value, e.g $\frac{2}{6} = \frac{1}{3}$.

F

factor

Numbers that divide exactly into a number are its factors, e.g. the factors of 12 are 1, 2, 3, 4, 6, 12.

frequency table

A table showing how often something occurs.

Type of pet	Tally	Frequency
Dog	卌 卌 l	11
Cat	卌 l	6
Goldfish	卌 ll	7
Budgie	lll	3

G

greatest value, least value

The highest or lowest value that can occur.

H

heptagon

A 2-D shape with seven straight sides.

hundred thousand

100 000.

hundredths

A fraction $\frac{1}{100}$ or 0.01.

I

integer, positive, negative

An integer is a whole number which can be positive or negative, e.g. –4, –2, 4, 100.

inverse

Addition is the inverse of subtraction, e.g. 16 + 24 = 40, 40 – 24 = 16. Multiplication is the inverse of division, e.g. 4 × 12 = 48, 48 ÷ 12 = 4.

irregular

Not regular. A shape with sides and angles that are not equal.

isosceles triangle

A triangle with 2 equal sides and 2 equal base angles.

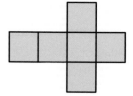

K

kilometre

A metric measure of distance. 1 km = 1000 m.

kite

A quadrilateral with adjacent sides that are equal.

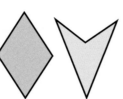

M

mass

A measure of the amount of matter in an object. Measured in grams (g), kilograms (kg) or tonnes (t).

measuring cylinder

A graduated cylinder for measuring volume and capacity accurately.

millennium

A thousand years (10 centuries).

millilitre

Symbol: ml. A measure of capacity. 1000 millilitres = 1 litre.

millimetre

Symbol: mm. A measure of length. 10 millimetres = 1 centimetres.

million

1 000 000.

minuend

The starting number in a subtraction calculation, e.g. 10 (the minuend) – 3 (the subtrahend) = 7 (the difference). See also *subtrahend, difference*.

minus

Another word for subtraction. The symbol – shows a negative number. See also *above/below zero*.

multiple

A multiple is the product of 2 numbers, e.g. the multiples of 7 are 7, 14, 21, 28 and so on.

multiplicand

A number to be multiplied, e.g. in 6 × 3 = 18, 6 is the multiplicand. See also *multiplier*.

multiplier

The multiplying number, e.g. in 6 × 3 = 18, 3 is the multiplier. See also *multiplicand*.

N

negative numbers

Numbers below zero. See also *integer, positive, negative*.

net

A pattern that you can cut out and fold to make a 3-D shape.

numerator

The number above the vinculum in a fraction. See also *denominator*.

O

oblong

An irregular rectangle. A 2-D shape with 2 pairs of opposite sides that are equal and the angles are 90°.

obtuse angle

An angle between 90° and 180°. See also *acute, reflex angle*.

P

parallelogram

A 2-D shape with 2 pairs of opposite sides that are equal and parallel. A rectangle is a special parallelogram with all the angles 90°.

polygon

The general name for 2-D shapes with straight sides. Includes triangle (3 sides), quadrilateral (4 sides), pentagon (5 sides) and so on.

polyhedron

The general name for 3-D shapes with straight sides. Plural polyhedra. Includes tetrahedron, prisms, pyramids, and so on.

prism

A 3-D shape with 2 identical and parallel ends, joined by rectangular faces. The cross-section of a prism is always the same as the ends.

prism

product

The result of multiplying 2 numbers. The product of 4 and 3 is 4 × 3 = 12.

Q

quadrilateral

A 2-D shape with 4 straight lines.

questionnaire

A set of questions given to people to fill in, in order to collect data for analysis. See also *survey*, *data*.

quotient

The answer to a division calculation, e.g. in 12 ÷ 6 = 2, 2 is the quotient. See also *dividend*.

dividend
$$12 \div 6 = 2 \leftarrow \text{quotient}$$
divisor

R

rectilinear

When all sides meet at right angles.

reflect, reflection

To transform an object by reflecting it in a mirror line. The image is the same shape and size as the object.

regular

A 2-D shape with all the sides equal length and equal angles.

rhombus

A 2-D shape with 4 equal sides, equal opposite angles.

right-angled triangle

A triangle with 1 right angle. Can be *isosceles* or *scalene*.

rotate, rotation

To transform an object by turning it in a given direction.

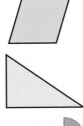

S

scalene triangle

A triangle with no equal sides or angles.

sphere, spherical

A sphere has a curved surface, where every point is the same distance from the centre. A ball-shape.

square centimetre (cm²)

A unit of measure of area equivalent to a square 1 cm by 1 cm. Symbol: cm².

square number, squared

A square number is a number that is multiplied by itself, e.g. $1 \times 1 + 1$, $2 \times 2 = 4$, $3 \times 3 = 9$.

subtrahend

The number that is subtracted from the minuend. See also *minuend*, *difference*.

sum

The answer to an addition calculation. The sum of 4 and 5 is 9. See also *total*.

survey

A survey collects data for analysis. See also *questionnaire*, *data*.

T

ten thousand

10 000.

tetrahedron

A 3-D shape with 4 triangular faces.

thousand less/more

The number one thousand whole units more or less than another number. 9000 is a thousand less than 10 000 and 11 000 is a thousand more than 10 000.

timetable

A table listing start and finish or arrival and departure times of activities or events, e.g. a school timetable or a public transport timetable.

total

The answer to an addition calculation. The total of 4, 3 and 5 is 12. See also *sum*.

translate, translation

To transform an object by moving it a given distance and direction. The image is the same shape and size as the object and in the same orientation.

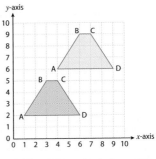

trapezium

A quadrilateral with
1 pair of parallel sides.

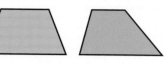

triangular

Like a triangle, a 2-D shape with 3 straight sides.

V

vinculum

The line that separates
the numerator and
denominator
in a fraction.

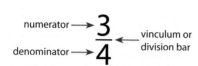

W

weight

The force exerted on a mass by gravity. The units are units of
force (Newtons). Often confused with *mass*.

whole-part relationship

Parts of the whole. In the fraction $\frac{2}{3}$, the whole has been
divided into 3 equal parts and we are thinking about 2 of
those parts. When thinking of an addition calculation, e.g.
$54 + 46 = 100$, 54 and 46 are the parts and 100 is the whole.
There are many whole-part relationships in mathematics.

X

x-axis

The horizontal line on a graph or coordinate grid that runs
through zero.

Y

y-axis

The vertical line on a graph or coordinate grid that runs
through zero.